DATE DUE FOR RETURN

THE MOMENT
AND OTHER ESSAYS

BY VIRGINIA WOOLF

Fiction

KEW GARDENS
THE VOYAGE OUT
NIGHT AND DAY
JACOB'S ROOM
MRS. DALLOWAY
TO THE LIGHTHOUSE
ORLANDO
THE WAVES
THE YEARS
BETWEEN THE ACTS
A HAUNTED HOUSE

Biography

FLUSH
ROGER FRY
VIRGINIA WOOLF AND
LYTTON STRACHEY: LETTERS

Criticism, etc.

THE COMMON READER: FIRST SERIES
THE COMMON READER: SECOND SERIES
CONTEMPORARY WRITERS
A ROOM OF ONE'S OWN
THREE GUINEAS
THE DEATH OF THE MOTH
THE MOMENT
THE CAPTAIN'S DEATH BED
GRANITE AND RAINBOW

Memoirs

A WRITER'S DIARY
MOMENTS OF BEING
THE DIARY OF VIRGINIA WOOLF
THE LETTERS OF VIRGINIA WOOLF

THE MOMENT
AND OTHER ESSAYS

Virginia Woolf

LONDON
THE HOGARTH PRESS
1981

Published by
The Hogarth Press Ltd
40 William IV Street
London WC2

*

Clarke, Irwin & Co. Ltd
Toronto

ISBN 0 7012 0271 8

First published 1947
Fourth impression 1981

Printed and bound in Great Britain by
Redwood Burn Limited
Trowbridge & Esher

Contents

5

CONTENTS

6

Editorial Note

IN my editorial note to *The Death of the Moth* I wrote that Virginia Woolf " left behind her a considerable number of essays, sketches, and short stories, some unpublished and some previously published in newspapers; there are, indeed, enough to fill three or four volumes". Since then the short stories have been published in *A Haunted House*. The present volume contains a further selection of essays. I have followed the same method of selection as in *The Death of the Moth*, including some of all the different kinds of essay—the sketch, literary criticism, biographical, "political"—and not attempting to choose according to some scale of merit or importance. The consequence is that the standard of achievement seems to me as high in this volume as it was in *The Common Reader* or in *The Death of the Moth*, and it is the same in the essays which I have not included, but are sufficient to fill yet another volume.

Some of the essays are now published for the first time; others have appeared in *The Times Literary Supplement, The Nation*, the *New Statesman and Nation, Time and Tide*, the *New York Saturday Review, New Writing*. I have included two essays with the same title, *Royalty*; the first was commissioned, but, for obvious reasons, not published by *Picture Post*; the second was published in *Time and Tide*.

What I said with regard to the unrevised state of the essays in the editorial note to *The Death of the Moth* applies to the essays included in this volume. If Virginia Woolf had lived, she would have revised or rewritten nearly all of them. The essays differ considerably in their state of "finish". All which have actually been published in newspapers have been written and rewritten and revised, though there is no doubt that the process would have continued. Some of them—e.g. *On Re-reading Novels*—have in fact been revised and rewritten after publication with a view to inclusion in volume form. Others, e.g. *The Moment*, exist only in a much earlier stage,

7

a rather rough typescript heavily corrected in handwriting. I have printed these exactly as they were left, except for punctuation and the correction of obvious mistakes, but I have done so with some hesitation, if only because the handwriting is occasionally extremely difficult to decipher.

LEONARD WOOLF

The Moment: Summer's Night

THE night was falling so that the table in the garden among the trees grew whiter and whiter; and the people round it more indistinct. An owl, blunt, obsolete looking, heavy weighted, crossed the fading sky with a black spot between its claws. The trees murmured. An aeroplane hummed like a piece of plucked wire. There was also, on the roads, the distant explosion of a motor cycle, shooting further and further away down the road. Yet what composed the present moment? If you are young, the future lies upon the present, like a piece of glass, making it tremble and quiver. If you are old, the past lies upon the present, like a thick glass, making it waver, distorting it. All the same, everybody believes that the present is something, seeks out the different elements in this situation in order to compose the truth of it, the whole of it.

To begin with: it is largely composed of visual and of sense impressions. The day was very hot. After heat, the surface of the body is opened, as if all the pores were open and everything lay exposed, not sealed and contracted, as in cold weather. The air wafts cold on the skin under one's clothes. The soles of the feet expand in slippers after walking on hard roads. Then the sense of the light sinking back into darkness seems to be gently putting out with a damp sponge the colour in one's own eyes. Then the leaves shiver now and again, as if a ripple of irresistible sensation ran through them, as a horse suddenly ripples its skin.

But this moment is also composed of a sense that the legs of the chair are sinking through the centre of the earth, passing through the rich garden earth; they sink, weighted down. Then the sky loses its colour perceptibly and a star here and there makes a point of light. Then changes, unseen in the day, coming in succession seem to make an order evident. One becomes aware that we are spectators and also passive participants in a pageant. And as nothing can interfere with the

9

order, we have nothing to do but accept, and watch Now little sparks, which are not steady, but fitful as if somebody were doubtful, come across the field. Is it time to light the lamp, the farmers' wives are saying: can I see a little longer? The lamp sinks down; then it burns up. All doubt is over. Yes the time has come in all cottages, in all farms, to light the lamps. Thus then the moment is laced about with these weavings to and fro, these inevitable downsinkings, flights, lamp lightings.

But that is the wider circumference of the moment. Here in the centre is a knot of consciousness; a nucleus divided up into four heads, eight legs, eight arms, and four separate bodies. They are not subject to the law of the sun and the owl and the lamp. They assist it. For sometimes a hand rests on the table; sometimes a leg is thrown over a leg. Now the moment becomes shot with the extraordinary arrow which people let fly from their mouths—when they speak.

"He'll do well with his hay."

The words let fall this seed, but also, coming from that obscure face, and the mouth, and the hand so characteristically holding the cigarette, now hit the mind with a wad, then explode like a scent suffusing the whole dome of the mind with its incense, flavour; let fall, from their ambiguous envelope, the self-confidence of youth, but also its urgent desire, for praise, and assurance; if they were to say: "But you're no worse looking than many—you're no different—people don't mark you out to laugh at you": that he should be at once so cock-a-hoop and so ungainly makes the moment rock with laughter, and with the malice that comes from overlooking other people's motives; and seeing what they keep hid; and so that one takes sides; he will succeed; or no he won't; and then again, this success, will it mean my defeat; or won't it? All this shoots through the moment, makes it quiver with malice and amusement; and the sense of watching and comparing; and the quiver meets the shore, when the owl flies out, and puts a stop to this judging, this overseeing, and with our wings spread, we too fly, take wing, with the owl, over the earth and survey the quietude of what sleeps, folded, slumbering, arm stretching in the vast dark and sucking its thumb too; the amorous and the innocent; and a sigh goes up. Could we not fly too, with broad wings and with softness; and be all one wing; all embracing, all gathering, and these boundaries, these pryings over hedge into hidden compartments of different colours be all swept into one colour by the brush of the wing; and so visit in splendour, augustly, peaks; and there lie exposed, bare, on the spine, high up, to the cold light of the moon rising, and when the moon rises, single, solitary, behold her, one, eminent over us?

Ah, yes, if we could fly, fly, fly. . . . Here the body is gripped; and shaken; and the throat stiffens; and the nostrils tingle; and like a rat shaken by a terrier one sneezes; and the whole universe is shaken; mountains, snows, meadows; moon; higgledy, piggledy, upside down, little splinters flying; and the head is jerked up, down. "Hay fever—what a noise!—there's no cure. Except spending hay time on a boat. Perhaps worse than the disease, though that's what a man did—crossing and recrossing, all the summer."

Issuing from a white arm, a long shape, lying back, in a film of black and white, under the tree, which, down sweeping, seems a part of that curving, that flowing, the voice, with its ridicule and its sense, reveals to the shaken terrier its own insignificance. No longer part of the snow; no part of the mountain; not in the least venerable to other human beings; but ridiculous; a little accident; a thing to be laughed at; discriminated out; seen clearly cut out, sneezing, sneezing, judged and compared. Thus into the moment steals self-assertion; ah, the sneeze again; the desire to sneeze with conviction; masterfully; making oneself heard; felt; if not pitied, then somebody of importance; perhaps to break away and go. But no; the other shape has sent from its arrow another fine binding thread, "Shall I fetch my Vapex?" She, the observant, the discriminating, who keeps in mind always other instances, so that there is nothing singular in any special case—who refuses to be jumped into extravagance; and so sceptical withal; cannot believe in miracles; sees the vanity of effort there; perhaps then it would be well to try here; yet if she isolates cases from the mists of hugeness, sees what is there all the more definitely; refuses to be bamboozled; yet in this definite discrimination shows some amplitude. That is why the moment becomes harder, is intensified, diminished, begins to be stained by some expressed personal juice; with the desire to be loved, to be held close to the other shape; to put off the veil of darkness and see burning eyes.

Then a light is struck; in it appears a sunburnt face, lean, blue-eyed, and the arrow flies as the match goes out:

"He beats her every Saturday; from boredom, I should say; not drink; there's nothing else to do."

The moment runs like quicksilver on a sloping board into the cottage parlour; there are the tea things on the table; the hard windsor chairs; tea caddies on the shelf for ornament; the medal under a glass shade; vegetable steam curling from the pot; two children crawling on the floor; and Liz comes in and John catches her a blow on the side of her head as she slopes past him, dirty, with her hair loose and one hairpin sticking out about to fall. And she moans in a chronic animal way; and the children look up and then make a whistling noise to imitate the engine which they trail across the flags; and John sits himself down with a thump at the table and carves a hunk of bread and munches because there is nothing to be done. A steam rises from his cabbage patch. Let us do something then, something to end this horrible moment, this plausible glistening moment that reflects in its smooth sides this intolerable kitchen, this squalor; this woman moaning; and the rattle of the toy on the flags, and the man munching. Let us smash it by breaking a match. There—snap.

And then comes the low of the cows in the field; and another cow to the left answers; and all the cows seem to be moving tranquilly across the field and the owl flutes off its watery bubble. But the sun is deep below the earth. The trees are growing heavier, blacker; no order is perceptible; there is no sequence in these cries, these movements; they come from no bodies; they are cries to the left and to the right. Nothing can be seen. We can only see ourselves as outlines, cadaverous, sculpturesque. And it is more difficult for the voice to carry through this dark. The dark has stripped the fledge from the arrow—the vibrations that rise red shiver as it passes through us.

Then comes the terror, the exultation; the power to rush out unnoticed, alone; to be consumed; to be swept away to become a rider on the random wind; the tossing wind; the trampling and neighing wind; the horse with the blown-back mane; the tumbling, the foraging; he who gallops for ever, nowhither travelling, indifferent; to be part of the eyeless dark, to be rippling and streaming, to feel the glory run molten up the spine, down the limbs, making the eyes glow, burning, bright, and penetrate the buffeting waves of the wind.

"Everything's sopping wet. It's the dew off the grass. Time to go in."

And then one shape heaves and surges and rises, and we pass, trailing coats, down the path towards the lighted windows, the dim glow behind the branches, and so enter the door, and the square draws its lines round us, and here is a chair, a table, glasses, knives, and thus we are boxed and housed, and will soon require a draught of soda-water and to find something to read in bed.

On Being Ill

CONSIDERING how common illness is, how tremendous the spiritual change that it brings, how astonishing, when the lights of health go down, the undiscovered countries that are then disclosed, what wastes and deserts of the soul a slight attack of influenza brings to view, what precipices and lawns sprinkled with bright flowers a little rise of temperature reveals, what ancient and obdurate oaks are uprooted in us by the act of sickness, how we go down into the pit of death and feel the waters of annihilation close above our heads and wake thinking to find ourselves in the presence of the angels and the harpers when we have a tooth out and come to the surface in the dentist's arm-chair and confuse his "Rinse the mouth—rinse the mouth" with the greeting of the Deity stooping from the floor of Heaven to welcome us—when we think of this, as we are so frequently forced to think of it, it becomes strange indeed that illness has not taken its place with love and battle and jealousy among the prime themes of literature. Novels, one would have thought, would have been devoted to influenza; epic poems to typhoid; odes to pneumonia; lyrics to toothache. But no; with a few exceptions—De Quincey attempted something of the sort in *The Opium Eater*; there must be a volume or two about disease scattered through the pages of Proust—literature does its best to maintain that its concern is with the mind; that the body is a sheet of plain glass through which the soul looks straight and clear, and, save for one or two passions such as desire and greed, is null, and negligible and non-existent. On the contrary, the very opposite is true. All day, all night the body intervenes; blunts or sharpens, colours or discolours, turns to wax in the warmth of June, hardens to tallow in the murk of February. The creature within can only gaze through the pane—smudged or rosy; it cannot separate off from the body like the sheath of a knife or

First published in 1930

the pod of a pea for a single instant; it must go through the whole unending procession of changes, heat and cold, comfort and discomfort, hunger and satisfaction, health and illness, until there comes the inevitable catastrophe; the body smashes itself to smithereens, and the soul (it is said) escapes. But of all this daily drama of the body there is no record. People write always of the doings of the mind; the thoughts that come to it; its noble plans; how the mind has civilised the universe. They show it ignoring the body in the philosopher's turret; or kicking the body, like an old leather football, across leagues of snow and desert in the pursuit of conquest or discovery. Those great wars which the body wages with the mind a slave to it, in the solitude of the bedroom against the assault of fever or the oncome of melancholia, are neglected. Nor is the reason far to seek. To look these things squarely in the face would need the courage of a lion tamer; a robust philosophy; a reason rooted in the bowels of the earth. Short of these, this monster, the body, this miracle, its pain, will soon make us taper into mysticism, or rise, with rapid beats of the wings, into the raptures of transcendentalism. The public would say that a novel devoted to influenza lacked plot; they would complain that there was no love in it—wrongly however, for illness often takes on the disguise of love, and plays the same odd tricks. It invests certain faces with divinity, sets us to wait, hour after hour, with pricked ears for the creaking of a stair, and wreathes the faces of the absent (plain enough in health, Heaven knows) with a new significance, while the mind concocts a thousand legends and romances about them for which it has neither time nor taste in health. Finally, to hinder the description of illness in literature, there is the poverty of the language. English, which can express the thoughts of Hamlet and the tragedy of Lear, has no words for the shiver and the headache. It has all grown one way. The merest schoolgirl, when she falls in love, has Shakespeare or Keats to speak her mind for her; but let a ufferer try to describe a pain in his head to a doctor and language at once runs dry. There is nothing ready made for him. He is forced to coin words himself, and, taking his pain in one hand, and a lump of pure sound in the other (as perhaps the people of Babel did in the beginning), so to crush them together that a brand new word in the end drops out. Probably it will be something laughable. For who of English birth can take liberties with the language? To us it is a sacred thing and therefore doomed to die, unless the Americans, whose genius is so much happier in the making of new words than in the disposition of the old, will come to our help and set the springs aflow. Yet it is not only a new language that we need, more primitive, more sensual, more obscene, but a new hierarchy of the passions; love must be deposed in favour of a temperature of 104; jealousy give place to the pangs of sciatica; sleeplessness play the part of villain, and the hero become a white liquid with a sweet taste—that mighty Prince with the moths' eyes and the feathered feet, one of whose names is Chloral.

But to return to the invalid. "I am in bed with influenza" —but what does that convey of the great experience; how the world has changed its shape; the tools of business grown remote; the sounds of festival become romantic like a merry-go-round heard across far fields; and friends have changed, some putting on a strange beauty, others deformed to the squatness of toads, while the whole landscape of life lies remote and fair, like the shore seen from a ship far out at sea, and he is now exalted on a peak and needs no help from man or God, and now grovels supine on the floor glad of a kick from a housemaid—the experience cannot be imparted and, as is always the way with these dumb things, his own suffering serves but to wake memories in his friends' minds of *their* influenzas, *their* aches and pains which went unwept last February, and now cry aloud, desperately, clamorously, for the divine relief of sympathy.

But sympathy we cannot have. Wisest Fate says no. If her children, weighted as they already are with sorrow, were to take on them that burden too, adding in imagination other pains to their own, buildings would cease to rise; roads would peter out into grassy tracks; there would be an end of music and of painting; one great sigh alone would rise to Heaven, and the only attitudes for men and women would be those of horror and despair. As it is, there is always some little distraction—an organ grinder at the corner of the hospital, a shop with book or trinket to decoy one past the prison or the workhouse, some absurdity of cat or dog to prevent one from turning the old beggar's hieroglyphic of misery into volumes of sordid suffering; and thus the vast effort of sympathy which those barracks of pain and discipline, those dried symbols of sorrow, ask us to exert on their behalf, is uneasily shuffled off for another time. Sympathy nowadays is dispensed chiefly by the laggards and failures, women for the most part (in whom the obsolete exists so strangely side by side with anarchy and newness), who, having dropped out of the race, have time to spend upon fantastic and unprofitable excursions; C. L. for example, who, sitting by the stale sickroom fire, builds up, with touches at once sober and imaginative, the nursery fender, the loaf, the lamp, barrel organs in the street, and all the simple old wives' tales of pinafores and escapades; A. R., the rash, the magnanimous, who, if you fancied a giant tortoise to solace you or a theorbo to cheer you, would ransack the markets of London and procure them somehow, wrapped in paper, before the end of the day; the frivolous K. T., who, dressed in silks and feathers, powdered and painted (which takes time too) as if for a banquet of Kings and Queens, spends her whole brightness in the gloom of the sick room, and makes the medicine bottles ring and the flames shoot up with her gossip and her mimicry. But such follies have had their day; civilisation points to a different goal; and then what place will there be for the tortoise and the theorbo?

There is, let us confess it (and illness is the great confessional), a childish outspokenness in illness; things are said, truths blurted out, which the cautious respectability of health conceals. About sympathy for example—we can do without it. That illusion of a world so shaped that it echoes every groan, of human beings so tied together by common needs and fears that a twitch at one wrist jerks another, where however strange your experience other people have had it too, where however far you travel in your own mind someone has been there before you—is all an illusion. We do not know our own souls, let alone the souls of others. Human beings do not go hand in hand the whole stretch of the way. There is a virgin forest in each; a snowfield where even the print of birds' feet is unknown. Here we go alone, and like it better so. Always to have sympathy, always to be accompanied, always to be understood would be

TRUE intolerable. But in health the genial pretence must be kept up
and the effort renewed—to communicate, to civilise, to share,
to cultivate the desert, educate the native, to work together by
day and by night to sport. In illness this make-believe ceases.
Directly the bed is called for, or, sunk deep among pillows in
one chair, we raise our feet even an inch above the ground on
another, we cease to be soldiers in the army of the upright;
we become deserters. They march to battle. We float with the
sticks on the stream; helter-skelter with the dead leaves on
the lawn, irresponsible and disinterested and able, perhaps for
the first time for years, to look round, to look up—to look, for
example, at the sky.

The first impression of that extraordinary spectacle is
strangely overcoming. Ordinarily to look at the sky for any
length of time is impossible. Pedestrians would be impeded and
disconcerted by a public sky-gazer. What snatches we get of it
are mutilated by chimneys and churches, serve as a background
for man, signify wet weather or fine, daub windows gold, and,
filling in the branches, complete the pathos ∴ ̄ dishevelled
autumnal plane trees in autumnal squares. Now, lying recumbent, staring straight up, the sky is discovered to be something
so different from this that really it is a little shocking. This then
has been going on all the time without our knowing it!—this
incessant making up of shapes and casting them down, this
buffeting of clouds together, and drawing vast trains of ships
and waggons from North to South, this incessant ringing up
and down of curtains of light and shade, this interminable
experiment with gold shafts and blue shadows, with veiling the
sun and unveiling it, with making rock ramparts and wafting
them away—this endless activity, with the waste of Heaven
knows how many million horse power of energy, has been left
to work its will year in year out. The fact seems to call for comment and indeed for censure. Ought not some one to write to
The Times? Use should be made of it. One should not let this
gigantic cinema play perpetually to an empty house. But watch
a little longer and another emotion drowns the stirrings of civic
ardour. Divinely beautiful it is also divinely heartless. Im-
measurable resources are used for some purpose which has
nothing to do with human pleasure or human profit. If we were

all laid prone, stiff, still the sky would be experimenting with its blues and its golds. Perhaps then, if we look down at something very small and close and familiar, we shall find sympathy. Let us examine the rose. We have seen it so often flowering in bowls, connected it so often with beauty in its prime, that we have forgotten how it stands, still and steady, throughout an entire afternoon in the earth. It preserves a demeanour of perfect dignity and self-possession. The suffusion of its petals is of inimitable rightness. Now perhaps one deliberately falls; now all the flowers, the voluptuous purple, the creamy, in whose waxen flesh the spoon has left a swirl of cherry juice; gladioli; dahlias; lilies, sacerdotal, ecclesiastical; flowers with prim cardboard collars tinged apricot and amber, all gently incline their heads to the breeze—all, with the exception of the heavy sunflower, who proudly acknowledges the sun at midday and perhaps at midnight rebuffs the moon. There they stand; and it is of these, the stillest, the most self-sufficient of all things that human beings have made companions; these that symbolise their passions, decorate their festivals, and lie (as if *they* knew sorrow) upon the pillows of the dead. Wonderful to relate, poets have found religion in nature; people live in the country to learn virtue from plants. It is in their indifference that they are comforting. That snowfield of the mind, where man has not trodden, is visited by the cloud, kissed by the falling petal, as, in another sphere, it is the great artists, the Miltons and the Popes, who console not by their thought of us but by their forgetfulness.

Meanwhile, with the heroism of the ant or the bee, however indifferent the sky or disdainful the flowers, the army of the upright marches to battle. Mrs. Jones catches her train. Mr. Smith mends his motor. The cows are driven home to be milked. Men thatch the roof. The dogs bark. The rooks, rising in a net, fall in a net upon the elm trees. The wave of life flings itself out indefatigably. It is only the recumbent who know what, after all, Nature is at no pains to conceal—that she in the end will conquer; heat will leave the world; stiff with frost we shall cease to drag ourselves about the fields; ice will lie thick upon factory and engine; the sun will go out. Even so, when the whole earth is sheeted and slippery, some undulation, some irregularity of surface will mark the boundary of an ancient garden, and there, thrusting its head up undaunted in the starlight, the rose will flower, the crocus will burn. But with the hook of life still in us still we must wriggle. We cannot stiffen peaceably into glassy mounds. Even the recumbent spring up at the mere imagination of frost about the toes and stretch out to avail themselves of the universal hope—Heaven, Immortality. Surely, since men have been wishing all these ages, they will have wished something into existence; there will be some green isle for the mind to rest on even if the foot cannot plant itself there. The co-operative imagination of mankind must have drawn some firm outline. But no. One opens the *Morning Post* and reads the Bishop of Lichfield on Heaven. One watches the church-goers file into those gallant temples where, on the bleakest day, in the wettest fields, lamps will be burning, bells will be ringing, and however the autumn leaves may shuffle and the winds sigh outside, hopes and desires will be changed to beliefs and certainties within. Do they look serene? Are their eyes filled with the light of their supreme conviction? Would one of them dare leap straight into Heaven off Beachy Head? None but a simpleton would ask such questions; the little company of believers lags and drags and strays. The mother is worn; the father tired. As for imagining Heaven, they have no time. Heaven-making must be left to the imagination of the poets. Without their help we can but trifle—imagine Pepys in Heaven, adumbrate little interviews with celebrated people on tufts of thyme, soon fall into gossip about such of our friends as have stayed in Hell, or, worse still, revert again to earth and choose, since there is no harm in choosing, to live over and over, now as man, now as woman, as sea-captain, or court lady, as Emperor or farmer's wife, in splendid cities and on remote moors, at the time of Pericles or Arthur, Charlemagne or George the Fourth—to live and live till we have lived out those embryo lives which attend about us in early youth until "I" suppressed them. But "I" shall not, if wishing can alter it, usurp Heaven too, and condemn us, who have played our parts here as William or Alice, to remain William or Alice for ever. Left to ourselves we speculate thus carnally. We need the poets to imagine for us. The duty of Heaven-

20

making should be attached to the office of the Poet Laureate. Indeed it is to the poets that we turn. Illness makes us disinclined for the long campaigns that prose exacts. We cannot command all our faculties and keep our reason and our judgment and our memory at attention while chapter swings on top of chapter, and, as one settles into place, we must be on the watch for the coming of the next, until the whole structure —arches, towers, and battlements—stands firm on its foundations. *The Decline and Fall of the Roman Empire* is not the book for influenza, nor *The Golden Bowl* nor *Madame Bovary*. On the other hand, with responsibility shelved and reason in the abeyance—for who is going to exact criticism from an invalid or sound sense from the bed-ridden?—other tastes assert themselves; sudden, fitful, intense. We rifle the poets of their flowers. We break off a line or two and let them open in the depths of the mind:

> *and oft at eve*
> *Visits the herds along the twilight meadows*

> *wandering in thick flocks along the mountains*
> *Shepherded by the slow unwilling wind.*

Or there is a whole three volume novel to be mused over in a verse of Hardy's or a sentence of La Bruyère. We dip in Lamb's Letters—some prose writers are to be read as poets—and find "I am a sanguinary murderer of time, and would kill him inchmeal just now. But the snake is vital", and who shall explain the delight? or open Rimbaud and read

> *O saisons o châteaux*
> *Quelle âme est sans défauts?*

and who shall rationalise the charm? In illness words seem to possess a mystic quality. We grasp what is beyond their surface meaning, gather instinctively this, that, and the other—a sound, a colour, here a stress, there a pause—which the poet, knowing words to be meagre in comparison with ideas, has strewn about his page to evoke, when collected, a state of mind which neither words can express nor the reason explain. Incomprehensibility has an enormous power over us in illness, more legitimately perhaps than the upright will allow. In health meaning has encroached upon sound. Our intelligence domineers over our senses. But in illness, with the police off duty, we creep beneath some obscure poem by Mallarmé or Donne, some phrase in Latin or Greek, and the words give out their scent and distil their flavour, and then, if at last we grasp the meaning, it is all the richer for having come to us sensually first, by way of the palate and the nostrils, like some queer odour. Foreigners, to whom the tongue is strange, have us at a disadvantage. The Chinese must know the sound of *Antony and Cleopatra* better than we do.

Rashness is one of the properties of illness—outlaws that we are—and it is rashness that we need in reading Shakespeare. It is not that we should doze in reading him, but that, fully conscious and aware, his fame intimidates and bores, and all the views of all the critics dull in us that thunder-clap of conviction which, if an illusion, is still so helpful an illusion, so prodigious a pleasure, so keen a stimulus in reading the great. Shakespeare is getting flyblown; a paternal government might well forbid writing about him, as they put his monument at Stratford beyond the reach of scribbling fingers. With all this buzz of criticism about, one may hazard one's conjectures privately, make one's notes in the margin; but, knowing that someone has said it before, or said it better, the zest is gone. Illness, in its kingly sublimity, sweeps all that aside and leaves nothing but Shakespeare and oneself. What with his overweening power and our overweening arrogance, the barriers go down, the knots run smooth, the brain rings and resounds with *Lear* or *Macbeth*, and even Coleridge himself squeaks like a distant mouse.

But enough of Shakespeare—let us turn to Augustus Hare. There are people who say that even illness does not warrant these transitions; that the author of *The Story of Two Noble Lives* is not the peer of Boswell; and if we assert that short of the best in literature we like the worst—it is mediocrity that is hateful—will have none of that either. So be it. The law is on the side of the normal. But for those who suffer a slight rise of temperature the names of Hare and Waterford and Canning ray out as beams of benignant lustre. Not, it is true, for the first hundred pages or so. There, as so often in these fat volumes, we flounder and threaten to sink in a plethora of aunts and uncles. We have to remind ourselves that there is such a thing as atmosphere; that the masters themselves often keep us waiting intolerably while they prepare our minds for whatever it may be—the surprise, or the lack of surprise. So Hare, too, takes his time; the charm steals upon us imperceptibly; by degrees we become almost one of the family, yet not quite, for our sense of the oddity of it all remains, and share the family dismay when Lord Stuart leaves the room—there was a ball going forward—and is next heard of in Iceland. Parties, he said, bored him—such were English aristocrats before marriage with intellect had adulterated the fine singularity of their minds. Parties bore them; they are off to Iceland. Then Beckford's mania for castle building attacked him; he must lift a French *château* across the Channel, and erect pinnacles and towers to use as servants' bedrooms at vast expense, upon the borders of a crumbling cliff, too, so that the housemaids saw their brooms swimming down the Solent, and Lady Stuart was much distressed, but made the best of it and began, like the high-born lady that she was, planting evergreens in the face of ruin. Meanwhile the daughters, Charlotte and Louisa, grew up in their incomparable loveliness, with pencils in their hands, for ever sketching, dancing, flirting, in a cloud of gauze. They are not very distinct it is true. For life then was not the life of Charlotte and Louisa. It was the life of families, of groups. It was a web, a net, spreading wide and enmeshing every sort of cousin, dependant, and old retainer. Aunts—Aunt Caledon, Aunt Mexborough—grandmothers—Granny Stuart, Granny Hardwicke—cluster in chorus, and rejoice and sorrow and eat Christmas dinner together, and grow very old and remain very upright, and sit in hooded chairs cutting flowers it seems out of coloured paper. Charlotte married Canning and went to India; Louisa married Lord Waterford and went to Ireland. Then letters begin to cross vast spaces in slow sailing ships and communication becomes still more protracted and verbose, and there seems no end to the space and the leisure of those early Victorian days, and faiths are lost and the life of Hedley Vicars revives them; aunts catch cold but recover; cousins marry;

there are the Irish famine and the Indian Mutiny, and both sisters remain to their great, but silent, grief without children to come after them. Louisa, dumped down in Ireland with Lord Waterford at the hunt all day, was often very lonely; but she stuck to her post, visited the poor, spoke words of comfort ("I am sorry indeed to hear of Anthony Thompson's loss of mind, or rather of memory; if, however, he can understand sufficiently to trust solely in our Saviour, he has enough") and sketched and sketched. Thousands of notebooks were filled with pen and ink drawings of an evening, and then the carpenter stretched sheets for her and she designed frescoes for schoolrooms, had live sheep into her bedroom, draped gamekeepers in blankets, painted Holy Families in abundance, until the great Watts exclaimed that here was Titian's peer and Raphael's master! At that Lady Waterford laughed (she had a generous, benignant sense of humour); and said that she was nothing but a sketcher; had scarcely had a lesson in her life—witness her angel's wings scandalously unfinished. Moreover, there was her father's house forever falling into the sea; she must shore it up; must entertain her friends; must fill her days with all sorts of charities, till her Lord came home from hunting, and then, at midnight often, she would sketch him with his knightly face half hidden in a bowl of soup, sitting with her sketch-book under a lamp beside him. Off he would ride again, stately as a crusader, to hunt the fox, and she would wave to him and think each time, what if this should be the last? And so it was, that winter's morning; his horse stumbled; he was killed. She knew it before they told her, and never could Sir John Leslie forget, when he ran downstairs on the day of the burial, the beauty of the great lady standing to see the hearse depart, nor, when he came back, how the curtain, heavy, mid-Victorian, plush perhaps, was all crushed together where she had grasped it in her agony.

The Faery Queen

THE FAERY QUEEN, it is said, has never been read to the end; no one has ever wished *Paradise Lost*, it is said, a word longer; and these remarks however exaggerated probably give pleasure, like a child's laugh at a ceremony, because they express something we secretly feel and yet try to hide. Dare we then at this time of day come out with the remark that *The Faery Queen* is a great poem? So one might say early rising, cold bathing, abstention from wine and tobacco are good; and if one said it, a blank look would steal over the company as they made haste to agree and then to lower the tone of the conversation. Yet it is true. Here are some general observations made by one who has gone through the experience, and wishes to urge others, who may be hiding their yawns and their polite boredom, to the same experience.

The first essential is, of course, not to read *The Faery Queen*. Put it off as long as possible. Grind out politics; absorb science; wallow in fiction; walk about London; observe the crowds; calculate the loss of life and limb; rub shoulders with the poor in markets; buy and sell; fix the mind firmly on the financial columns of the newspapers, weather; on the crops; on the fashions. At the mere mention of chivalry shiver and snigger; detest allegory; revel in direct speech; adore all the virtues of the robust, the plain spoken; and then, when the whole being is red and brittle as sandstone in the sun, make a dash for *The Faery Queen* and give yourself up to it.

But reading poetry is a complex art. The mind has many layers, and the greater the poem the more of these are roused and brought into action. They seem, too, to be in order. The faculty we employ upon poetry at the first reading is sensual; the eye of the mind opens. And Spenser rouses the eye softly and brilliantly with his green trees, his pearled women, his crested and plumed knights. (Then we need to use our sympathies, not the strong passions, but the simple wish to go with

25

our knight and his lady to feel their heat and cold, and their thirst and hunger.) And then we need movement. Their figures, as they pass along the grass track, must reach a hovel or a palace or find a man in weeds reading his book. That too is gratified. And then living thus with our eyes, with our legs and arms, with the natural quiet feelings of liking and disliking tolerantly and gently excited, we realise a more complex desire that all these emotions should combine. There must be a pervading sense of belief, or much of our emotion will be wasted. The tree must be part of the knight; the knight of the lady. All these states of mind must support one another, and the strength of the poem will come from the combination, just as it will fail if at any point the poet loses belief.

But it may be said, when a poet is dealing with Faery Land and the supernatural people who live there, belief can only be used in a special sense. We do not believe in the existence of giants and ogres, but in something that the poet himself believed them to represent. What then was Spenser's belief, when he wrote his poem? He has himself declared that the "general intention and meaning" of *The Faery Queen* was "to fashion a gentleman or noble person in vertuous and noble discipline". It would be absurd to pretend that we are more than intermittently conscious of the poet's meaning. Yet as we read, we half consciously have the sense of some pattern hanging in the sky, so that without referring any of the words to a special place, they have that meaning which comes from their being parts of a whole design, and not an isolated fragment of unrelated loveliness. The mind is being perpetually enlarged by the power of suggestion. Much more is imagined than is stated. And it is due to this quality that the poem changes, with time, so that after four hundred years it still corresponds to something which we, who are momentarily in the flesh, feel at the moment.

The question asks itself, then, how Spenser, himself imprisoned in so many impediments of circumstance, remote from us in time, in speech, in convention, yet seems to be talking about things that are important to us too? Compare, for example, his perfect gentleman with Tennyson's Arthur. Already, much in Tennyson's pattern is unintelligible; an easy butt for satire. Among living writers again, there is none who is able to display a typical figure. Each seems limited to one room of the human dwelling. But with Spenser, though here in this department of our being, we seem able to unlock the door and walk about. We miss certain intensities and details; but on the other hand we are uncabined. We are allowed to give scope to a number of interests, delights, curiosities, and loves that find no satisfaction in the poetry of our own time. But though it would be easy to frame a reason for this and to generalise about the decay of faith, the rise of machines, the isolation of the human being, let us, however, work from the opposite point of view. In reading *The Faery Queen* the first thing, we said, was that the mind has different layers. It brings one into play and then another. The desire of the eye, the desire of the body, desires for rhythm, movement, the desire for adventure—each is gratified. And this gratification depends upon the poet's own mobility. He is alive in all his parts. He scarcely seems to prefer one to another. We are reminded of the old myth of the body which has many organs, and the lesser and the obscure are as important as the kingly and important.

Here at any rate the poet's body seems all alive. A fearlessness, a simplicity that is like the movement of a naked savage possesses him. He is not merely a thinking brain; he is a feeling body, a sensitive heart. He has hands and feet, and, as he says himself, a natural chastity, so that some things are judged unfit for the pen. "My chaster muse for shame doth blush to write." In short, when we read *The Faery Queen*, we feel that the whole being is drawn upon, not merely a separate part.

To say this is to say that the conventions that Spenser uses are not enough to cut us off from the inner meaning. And the reason soon makes itself apparent. When we talk of the modern distaste for allegory, we are only saying that we prefer our qualities in another form. The novelist uses allegory; that is to say, when he wishes to expound his characters, he makes them think; Spenser impersonated his psychology. Thus if the novelist now wished to convey his hero's gloom, he would tell us his thoughts; Spenser creates a figure called Despair. He has the fullest sense of what sorrow is. But he typifies it; he creates a dwelling, an old man who comes out of

the house and says I cannot tell; and then the figure of Despair
with his beautiful elegy. Instead of being prisoned in one
breast we are shown the outer semblance. He is working thus
on a larger, freer, more depersonalised scale. By making the
passions into people, he gives them an amplitude. And who
shall say that this is the less natural, the less realistic? For the
most exact observer has to leave much of his people's minds
obscure.

Once we get him out of his private mythology, there is
no mythology which can personify his actions. We wish to
convey delight and have to describe an actual garden, here and
now; Spenser at once calls up a picture of nymphs dancing,
youth, maidens crowned. And yet it is not pictorial merely.
Nothing is more refreshing, nothing serves more to sting and
revive us than the spray of fresh hard words, little colloquialisms,
tart green words that might have been spoken at dinner,
joining in easily with the more stately tribe. But such exter-
nality is impossible to us, because we have lost our power to
create symbols. Spenser's ability to use despair in person
depends on his power to create a world in which such a figure
draws natural breath, living breath. He has his dwelling at the
centre of a universe which offers him the use of dragons,
knights, magic; and all the company that exist about them; and
flowers and dawn and sunset. All this was still just within his
reach. He could believe in it, his public could believe in it,
sufficiently to make it serviceable. It was, of course, just slipping
from his grasp. That is obvious from his own words. His poem,
he says, will be called the abundance of an idle brain.
His language, too, oddly compounded of the high flown and
the vernacular, was just then at the turn. On the one hand we
have the old smooth conventions—Tithonus, Cynthia, Phoebus,
and the rest; on the other fry and rascal and losel, the common
speech that was current on the lips of the women at the door.
He was not asking the reader to adopt an unnatural pose; only
to think poetically. And the writer's faith is still effective. We
are removed four hundred years from Spenser; and the effort
to think back into his mood requires some adjustment, some
oblivion; but there is nothing false in what is to be done; it is
easier to read Spenser than to read William Morris.

The true difficulty lies elsewhere. It lies in the fact that the poem is a meditation, not a dramatisation. At no point is Spenser under the necessity of bringing his characters to the surface; they lack the final embodiment which is forced so drastically upon the playwright. They sink back into the poet's mind and thus lack definition. He is talking about them; they are not using their own words. Hence the indistinctness which leads, as undoubtedly it does lead, to monotony. The verse becomes for a time a rocking horse; swaying up and down; a celestial rocking horse, whose pace is always rhythmical and seemly, but lulling, soporific. It sings us to sleep; it lulls the teeth of the wind. On no other terms, however, could we be kept in being. And to compensate we have the quality of that mind; the sense that we are confined in one continuous consciousness, which is Spenser's; that he has saturated and enclosed this world, that we live in a great bubble blown from the poet's brain. Yet if it ignores our own marks, houses, chimneys, roads, the multitudinous details which serve like signposts or features to indicate to us where our emotions lie, it is not a private world of fantasy. Here are the qualities that agitate living people at the moment; spite, greed, jealousy, ugliness, poverty, pain; Spenser in his poet's castle was as acutely aware of the rubs and tumbles of life as the living, but by virtue of his poetry blew them away into the higher air. So we feel not shut in, but freed; and take our way in a world which gives expression to sensation more vigorously, more exactly than we can manage for ourselves in the flesh. It is a world of astonishing physical brilliance and intensity; sharpened, intensified as objects are in a clearer air; such as we see them, not in dreams, but when all the faculties are alert and vigorous; when the stuffing and the detail have been brushed aside; and we see the bone and the symmetry; now in a landscape, in Ireland or in Greece; and now when we think of ourselves, under the more intense ray of poetry; under its sharper, its lovelier light.

Congreve's Comedies

THE four great plays through which Congreve is immortal take up very little space, and can be bought very cheaply; but they can be seen very seldom, and to read them, silently and in solitude, is to do them an injustice. The best way to repair that injustice is to consider them with the author's help more critically, if more coldly, than we are able when the words are embodied on the stage. Congreve, the man of mystery, the man of superb genius who ceased to use his genius at his height, was also, as any reader may guess from almost any page, of the class of writers who are not so entirely submerged in their gift but that they can watch it curiously and to some extent guide it even when they are possessed by it. Whatever he has to say in a letter, in a dedication, in a prologue about his art is worth listening to with all our ears. Let us then put to him some of the questions that the remembrance of his plays has left over in the mind before we allow the Tattles and the Foresights, the Wishforts and the Millamants to sweep us off our feet.

First there is the old grievance which, though it sounds elementary, must always have its say: the grievance that is summed up in the absurd names he gives his characters—Vainlove, Fondlewife, and the rest—as if we were back again in the age of mummer and cart, when one humour to one character was all the audience could grasp or the actor express. To that he replies, ". . . the distance of the stage requires the figures represented to be something larger than the life", a warning to the reader to suppress the desire for certain subtleties which the playwright cannot satisfy, a reminder that the imponderable suggestions which come together on silent feet in fiction are denied the playwright. He must speak; the speaking voice is the only instrument allowed him. That introduces a second question: they must speak, but why so artificially? Men and women were never so witty as he makes them; they never

Written in August 1937

speak so aptly, so instantly, and with such a wealth of figure and imagery as he would have us believe. And to that he replies, "I believe if a poet should steal a dialogue of any length, from the extempore discourse of the two wittiest men upon earth, he would find the scene but coldly receiv'd by the town". People on the stage must be larger than life because they are further from us than in the book; and cleverer than life because if he set down their actual words we should be bored to distraction. Every writer has his selection to make; his artifice to enforce; these are the playwright's. These are the methods by which he puts us in the frame of mind needed for his purpose.

Still there remains another grievance which is not so elementary nor so easily laid to rest; and that is, of course, the plot. Who can remember the plot when the book is shut? Who has not been teased by its intricacies while the book is open? As everybody is agreed something must happen, and it matters very little what happens if it serves to make the characters more real, or more profound, than they would otherwise have been; a plot should put the characters on the rack and show them thus extended. But what are we to say when the plot merely teases and distorts the character, and distracts us from any more profound enjoyment than that of asking who is behind that door, who is behind that mask? To this Congreve the critic gives us no satisfactory answer. Sometimes, as in the preface to *The Double Dealer*, he prides himself that he has maintained "the unities of the drama". But a certain doubt declares itself elsewhere. In the dedication to *The Way of the World* he envies Terence. Terence, he points out, had "great advantages to encourage his undertaking for he built most on the foundations of Menander; his plots were generally modelled and his characters ready drawn to his hand". Either then, one must conclude, the old weather-worn plots which slip into the mind so smoothly that we scarcely notice them—the legendary, the prehistoric— are the only tolerable ones, or we are forced to suppose that the plot-making genius is so seldom combined with the genius for creating character that we must allow even Shakespeare to fail here—even Shakespeare sometimes lets the plot dictate to the character; suffers the story to drag the character out of its natural orbit. And Congreve, who had not Shakespeare's miraculous fecundity, who could not cover up the farfetched and the mechanical with the abundance of his imagination and the splendour of his poetry, fails here. The character is squeezed to fit the situation; the machine has set its iron stamp upon live flesh and blood.

But, now that we have dismissed the questions that hang about an unopened book, let us submit ourselves to the dramatist in action. The dramatist is in action from the very first word on the very first page. There are no preliminaries, no introductions; the curtain rises and they are in the thick of it. Never was any prose so quick. Miraculously pat, on the spot, each speaker caps the last, without fumbling or hesitation; their minds are full charged; it seems as if they had to rein themselves in, bursting with energy as they are, alive and alert to their finger tips. It is we who fumble, make irrelevant observations, notice the chocolate or the cinnamon, the sword or the muslin, until the illusion takes hold of us, and what with the rhythm of the speech and the indescribable air of tension, of high breeding that pervades it, the world of the stage becomes the real world and the other, outside the play, but the husk and cast-off clothing. To attempt to reduce this first impression to words is as futile as to explain a physical sensation— the slap of a wave, the rush of wind, the scent of a bean field. It is conveyed by the curl of a phrase on the ear; by speed; by stillness. It is as impossible to analyse Congreve's prose as to distinguish the elements—the bark of a dog, the song of a bird, the drone of the branches—which make the summer air. But then, since words have meaning, we notice here a sudden depth beneath the surface, a meaning not grasped but felt, and then come to realise something not merely dazzling in this world, but natural, for all its wit; even familiar, and traditional. It has a coarseness, a humour something like Shakespeare's; a toppling imagination that heaps image upon image; a lightning swiftness of apprehension that snatches a dozen meanings and compacts them into one.

And yet it is not Shakespeare's world; for just as we think, tossed up on the crest of some wonderful extravagance of humour, to be swept into poetry we come slap against hard common sense, and realise that here is a different combination of elements from the poet's. There is tragedy—Lady Touchwood and Maskwell in *The Double Dealer* are not comic figures —but when tragedy and comedy collide it is comedy that wins. Lady Touchwood seizes her dagger; but she drops it. A moment more and it would have been too late. Already she has passed from prose to rant. Already we feel not that the scene is ridiculous, for there is passion there; but that it is unsafe. Congreve has lost his control, his fine balance is upset; he feels the ground tremble beneath him. Mr. Brisk's comment, "This is all very surprising, let me perish", is the appropriate one. With that he finds his feet and withdraws.

The world that we have entered, then, in Congreve's comedies is not the world of the elemental passions. It is an enclosure surrounded with the four walls of a living room. Ladies and gentlemen go through their figures with their tongues to the measure dictated by common sense as precisely as they dance the minuet with their feet; but the image has only a superficial rightness. We have only to compare Congreve's comedy with Goldsmith's or with Sheridan's, let alone with Wilde's, to be aware that if, to distinguish him from the Elizabethans, we confine him to a room, not a world, that room is not the drawing-room of the eighteenth century, still less is it the drawing-room of the nineteenth century. Drays roar on the cobbles beneath; the brawling of street hucksters and tavern rioters comes in at the open windows. There is a coarseness of language, an extravagance of humour, and a freedom of manners which cast us back to the Elizabethans. Yet it is in a drawing-room, surrounded by all the fopperies and refinements of the most sophisticated society in the world, that these ladies and gentlemen speak so freely, drink so deeply, and smell so strong. It is the contrast, perhaps, that makes us more aware of the coarseness of the Restoration dramatists than of the Elizabethan. A great lady who spits on the floor offends where a fishwife merely amuses. And perhaps it was for this reason that Congreve incurred first the majestic censure of Dr. Johnson and then the more supercilious contempt of the Victorians who neglected, Sir Edmund Gosse informs us, either to read him or to act him. More conscious than we are of the drawing-room, they were quicker repelled perhaps by any violation of its decencies.

But however we may account for the change, to reach *The Way of the World* through *The Old Bachelor*, *The Double Dealer*, and *Love for Love* is to become more and more at loggerheads with Dr. Johnson's dictum:

> It is acknowledged, with universal conviction, that the perusal of his works will make no man better; and that their ultimate effect is to represent pleasure in alliance with vice, and to relax those obligations by which life ought to be regulated.

On the contrary, to read Congreve's plays is to be convinced that we may learn from them many lessons much to our advantage both as writers of books and—if the division is possible—as livers of life. We might learn there, to begin with, the discipline of plain speech; to leave nothing lurking in the insidious shades of obscurity that can be said in words. The phrase is always finished; nothing is left to dwindle into darkness, to sound after the words are over. Then, when we have learnt to express ourselves, we may go on to observe the indefatigable hard work of a great writer: how he keeps us entertained because something is always happening, and on the alert because that something is always changing, and by contrasting laughter and seriousness, action and thought, keeps the edge of the emotions always sharp. To ring so many changes and keep up so rapid a speed of movement might well be enough, but in addition each of these characters has its own being, and each differs—the sea-dog from the fop, the old eccentric from the man of the world, the maid from the mistress. He has to enter into each; to leave his private pigeon-hole and invest himself with the emotions of another human being, so that speech meets speech at full tilt, each from its own angle.

A genius for phrase-making helps him. Now he strikes off a picture in a flash: ". . . there he lies with a great beard, like a Russian bear upon a drift of snow". Now in a marvellous rush of rapid invention he conveys a whole chapter of guttersnipe life.

> That I took from the washing of old gauze and weaving of dead hair, with a bleak blue nose, over a chafing dish

of starv'd embers, and dining behind a traverse rag, in a shop no bigger than a bird cage.

Then, again, like some miraculous magpie he repeats the naïve words, follows the crude emotions, of a great gawky girl like Miss Prue. However it is done, to enter into such diverse characters is, the moralists may note, at any rate to forget your own. Undoubtedly it is true that his language is often coarse; but then it is also true that his characters are more alive, quicker to strip off veils, more intolerant of circumlocutions than the ordinary run of people. They are reduced to phrase-making oftener than we could wish, and fine phrases often sound cynical; but then the situations are often so improbable that only fine phrases will cover them, and words, we must remember, were still to Congreve's generation as delightful as beads to a savage. Without that rapture the audacity of his splendid phrases would have been impossible.

But if we have to admit that some of the characters are immoral, and some of the opinions cynical, still we must ask how far we can call a character immoral or an opinion cynical if we feel that the author himself was aware of its immorality and intended its cynicism? And, though it is a delicate matter to separate an author from his characters and detach him from their opinions, no one can read Congreve's comedies without detecting a common atmosphere, a general attitude that holds them together for all their diversity. The stress laid on certain features creates a common likeness as unmistakable as the eyes and nose of a family face. The plays are veined through and through with satire. "Therefore I would rail in my writings and be revenged", says Valentine in *Love for Love*. Congreve's satire seems sometimes, as Scandal says, to have the whole world for its butt. Yet there is underneath a thinking mind, a mind that doubts and questions. Some hint thrown out in passing calls us back to make us ponder it: for instance, Mellefont's "Ay, My Lord, I shall have the same reason for happiness that your Lordship has, I shall think myself happy". Or, again, a sudden phrase like "There's comfort in a hand stretched out to one that's sinking" suggests, by its contrast, a sensibility that trembles on the edge of tears. Nothing is stressed; sentiment never broadens into sentimentality; everything passes as quickly as a ray of light and blends as indistinguishably. But if we needs must prove that the creator of Sir Sampson Legend and old Foresight had not only a prodigious sense of human absurdity and a bitter conviction of its insincerity but as quick a regard for its honesty and decency as any Victorian or Dr. Johnson himself, we need only point to his simplicity. After we have run up the scale of absurdity to its sublime heights a single word again and again recalls us to common sense. "That my poor father should be so very silly" is one such comment, immensely effective in its place. Again and again we are brought back to sanity and daylight by the sound of a voice speaking in its natural tones.

But it is the Valentines, the Mirabells, the Angelicas, and the Millamants who keep us in touch with truth and, by striking a sudden serious note, bring the rest to scale. They have sharpened their emotions upon their wits. They have flouted each other; bargained; taken love and examined it by the light of reason; teased and tested each other almost beyond endurance. But when it comes to the point and she must be serious, the swiftest of all heroines, whose mind and body seem equally winged, so that there is a rush in the air as she passes and we exclaim with Scandal. "Gone; why, she was never here, nor anywhere else", has a centre of stillness in her heart and enough emotion in her words to furbish out a dozen pages of eloquent disquisition. "Why does not the man take me? Would you have me give myself to you over again?" The words are simple, and yet, after what has already been said, so brimming with meaning that Mirabell's reply, "Ay, over and over again", seems to receive into itself more than words can say. And this depth of emotion, we have to reflect, the change and complexity that are implied in it, have been reached in the direct way; that is by making each character speak in his or her own person, without addition from the author or any soliloquy save such as can be spoken on the stage in the presence of an audience. No, whether we read him from the moralist's angle or from the artist's, to agree with Dr. Johnson is an impossibility. To read the comedies is not to "relax those obligations by which life ought to be regulated". On the contrary, the more slowly we read him and the more carefully, the more meaning we find, the more beauty we discover.

Here perhaps, in the reflections that linger when the book is shut and *The Way of the World* is finished, lies the answer to the old puzzle why at the height of his powers he stopped writing. It is that he had done all that was possible in that kind. The last play held more than any audience could grasp at a single sitting. The bodily presence of actors and actresses must, it would seem, often overpower the words that they had to speak. He had forgotten, or disregarded, his own axiom that "the distance of the stage requires the figures represented to be something larger than the life". He had written, as he says in the dedication, for "the *Few*", and "but little of it was prepar'd for that general taste which seems now to be predominant in the palates of our audience". He had come to despise his public, and it was time therefore either to write differently or to leave off. But the novel, which offered another outlet, was uncongenial; he was incorrigibly dramatic, as his one attempt at fiction shows. And poetry, too, was denied him, for though again and again he brings us to the edge of poetry in a phrase like "You're a woman, One to whom Heav'n gave beauty, when it grafted roses on a briar", and suggests, as Meredith does in his novels, the mood of poetry, he was unable to pass beyond human idiosyncrasy to the more general statement of poetry. He must move and laugh and bring us into touch with action instantly.

Since these two paths then were blocked, what other way was there for a writer of Congreve's temperament but to make an end? Dangerous as it is to distinguish a writer from his work, we cannot help but recognise a man behind the plays—a man as sensitive to criticism as he was skilled in inflicting it on others; for what is his defiance of the critics but deference to them? A scholar too with all the scholar's fastidiousness; a man of birth and breeding for whom the vulgar side of fame held little gratification; a man, in short, who might well have said with Valentine, "Nay, I am not violently bent upon the trade", and sit, handsome and portly and sedate as his portrait shows him, "very gravely with his hat over his eyes", as the gossips observed him, content to strive no more.

But indeed he left very little for the gossips to feed upon; no writer of his time and standing passed through the world more privately. Voltaire left a dubious anecdote; the Duchess of Marlborough, it is said, had an effigy of him set at her table after his death; his few discreet letters provide an occasional hint: "Ease and quiet is what I hunt after"; "I feel very sensibly and silently for those whom I love"—that is all. But there is a fitness in this very absence of relics as though he had consumed whatever was irrelevant to his work and left us to find him there. And there, indeed, we find something beyond himself; beyond the many figures of his fertile and brilliant imagination; beyond Tattle and Ben, Foresight and Angelica, Maskwell and Lady Wishfort, Mirabell and Mellefont and Millamant. Between them they have created what is not to be confined within the limits of a single character or expressed in any one play—a world where each part depends upon the other, the serene, impersonal, and indestructible world of art.

Sterne's Ghost

THAT men have ghosts; that ghosts revisit the places where life ran quickest; that Sterne therefore haunts no churchyard, but the room where *Tristram Shandy* was written—all this may be taken for granted; even if we find it no such easy matter to decide in what mood and with what motives the ghost of Sterne beat regularly at midnight upon the wall of Mrs. Simpson's best bedroom in Stonegate, Yorks.

Mrs. Simpson made no secret of the matter, which perhaps was too notorious to be concealed. Owing to the ghost, she told the young Mathews, she would let the rooms, large as they were and convenient for the theatre, very cheap indeed, and perceiving something in Mrs. Mathews's aspect which made her think her, as indeed she was, "a candidate for literary gains", she added how it was in this room and at that very table that a very famous book called *Tristram Shandy* was written, she believed, some forty years before. Even without its literary associations the cheapness of the lodging was enough to excuse the ghost, for the young Mathews were extremely poor—Charles acting at a salary of twenty-five shillings a week in Tate Wilkinson's company, but Tate did not scruple to tell him that with his screwed-up face and threadpaper body he had better keep a shop than go upon the stage, while poor Eliza, the girl whom Charles had married, out of pity, the second Mrs. Mathews said, without "*really* loving her", had not a penny to her name, which happened to be Strong. And Strong she had need to be, said Charles's father, strong in character, strong in health, strong in principles, strong in affections, if she became the wife of the misguided boy who so wantonly preferred the stage and all its evils to selling serious books to saintly personages in the Strand. But Eliza herself was conscious of one source of strength only (besides that she was very much in love with her husband) and that was her gift for

Written in 1925

39

writing—her passion for literature. When Mrs. Simpson at one and the same moment lowered the rent and mentioned Sterne, the bargain was struck and the rooms taken. The ghost must be endured.

That necessity arose, indeed, the very first night the Mathews went to bed. As York Minster struck the first chimes of midnight three powerful blows resounded on the wall at the back of the young couple's bed. The same thing happened night after night. York Minster had only to begin striking twelve and the ghost struck three. Watch was set; experiments were made; but whether it was the ghost of Sterne or the malevolence of some ill-wisher, no cause could be discovered and the young people could only move their bed, and shift their bedtime, which, as the playhouse hours were late and Charles had a passion for reading or talking late at night, was a matter of not much difficulty. Such courage could hardly have been expected of so frail a woman. But unfortunately Eliza had a reason for tolerating ghosts, if they reduced the rent, which she dared not tell her husband. Every week, like the honest and affectionate creature he was, he poured his salary—twenty-five shillings—into her lap, and every week she assured him that twenty-five shillings was ample—all their bills were paid. But every week a certain number, an increasing number, for all she could do to keep their expenses down, were slipped, unpaid, into Sterne's table drawer. Eliza perhaps had some inkling of the fact that her husband had married her impetuously in the goodness of his heart, from pity that the only child of the late Dr. Strong should have to support herself by inculcating the principles of arithmetic into the daughters of the gentlemen of Swansea. At any rate, she was determined that he should never suffer for his generosity. Comforts he must have, and if twenty-five shillings a week were not enough to pay for them she would pay for them herself out of her own earnings. She was confident that she could do it. She would write a novel, a novel like *Tristram Shandy* perhaps, save that her knowledge of life was unfortunately limited, which would set all London in a roar. And then she would come to her husband with the bills receipted and her deception confessed, and give him the proceeds of her famous novel to do what he liked with. But that day was still far distant—at present she must work. While Charles was acting and reading, while Charles, who loved talk and hated bedtime, was gossiping and chattering and taking off odd characters, so that he was famous in the green room whatever he might be upon the stage, Eliza wrote. She wrote every kind of piece—novels, sonnets, elegies, love songs. The publishers took them, the publishers printed them, but they never paid her a penny for them, and on she toiled, always carefully concealing her work from her husband, so that his surprise when the day of revelation came might be entire.

Meanwhile the bills accumulated, and act as Charles might (and there were some young ladies in York who thought him the finest comic actor they had ever seen, and would stand a whole evening in the wings to hear him) his salary remained twenty-five shillings and no more. It was useless for the ghost to knock; useless for Eliza's back to ache; useless for her good brother-in-law William to implore her to write everything twice over, peruse the best works of the best authors, and find mottoes for all her chapters—she had no choice; write she must. Surely the novel she was now engaged on—*What Has Been*—promised better than the others, and with a little help from William, who knew Mr. Wordsworth and could perhaps solicit the favours of reviewers, might, indeed must, bring her fame. Sitting where Sterne had sat, writing where Sterne had written, the omens were auspicious.

There, at any rate, long after the ghost had knocked thrice and York Minster had tolled twelve times, she sat writing. She neglected to take exercise. She never allowed herself to stand in the wings a whole evening to see her Charles in his comic parts. At last signs of exhaustion became apparent. Alarmed by her wasted looks, Charles brought a doctor to see her. But one glance was enough. Nothing could now be done. Whatever the cause, lack of exercise or lack of food, or whether the nervous strain of hearing those three taps delivered nightly had hopelessly injured her constitution, consumption was far advanced; and all the doctor could do was to prescribe apothecaries' stuff, which, expensive as it was, Charles feared to be useless.

Eliza was now confined to bed. Her projects had totally

failed. *What Has Been* appeared, but, even corrected and at least partially supplied with mottoes by the kindness of Mr. William Mathews, failed like its predecessors, and she was at an end of her resources. Even so, the worst was still to come. The butcher or the baker stopped Charles in the street and demanded payment. The drawer and its bills had to be revealed. The whole of her miserable, innocent, overwhelming deception must be confessed. Charles took the blow like an angel, said not a word of complaint, though the bills were to hang about his neck for years to come. And now, for the first time, the ghost fell silent. York Minster struck midnight and there was no reply. But really the silence was worse than the sound! To lie and wait for the three stout strokes as York Minster struck twelve, and then to hear nothing—that seemed to convey a more appalling message than the blow itself—as if the enemy had worked its will and gone its way. But this very silence inspired Eliza Mathews with a desperate courage. With the ghost quiescent, the novels unsold, the bills unpaid, Charles all day at the playhouse, often cast down by his failure and the thought of his father's displeasure—for the God-fearing book-seller in the Strand, where the whole house was hung with portraits of the Saints framed in ebony, and canting humbugs bamboozled the simple old tradesman out of his livelihood, had been justified in his warnings—with all this that she had caused, or failed to prevent, to oppress her, and the daily decline of her own health to appal, Eliza framed a terrible and desperate resolve. There was a girl at the playhouse for whom she had an affection, a singer who was friendless as Eliza herself had been, and timid and charming. For this young woman, Anne Jackson by name, Eliza sent. She was better, Eliza claimed, as Anne came in, and indeed her looks confirmed it; much better, because of an idea that had come to her, which she counted on her friend's help to carry out. First, before her husband came back, she wished to be propped up in bed, in order, she said mysteriously, "to be able to look at you both while I reveal my project". Directly Charles Mathews appeared, and exclaimed in his turn at her sparkle, her animation, she began. Sitting up, forced often to pause for breath, she said how she knew her fate; death was inevitable; how the thought of her husband's loneliness oppressed her—worse, the thought that he would marry again a woman who did not understand him. Here she paused exhausted, and Charles looked at Anne and Anne at Charles, as if to ask had she lost her reason? On she went again. It was even worse, she said, to think of Anne left in her youth and inexperience without such help as she, Eliza, might have given her. Thoughts of this kind embittered her last moments. Surely, then, they would grant the last request she would ever make? She took her husband's hand and kissed it; then took her friend's and kissed that too "in a solemn manner, which I remember made me tremble all over", and at last framed her terrible request. Would they, there and then, pledge themselves to marry each other when she was dead?

Both were flabbergasted. Anne burst into floods of tears. Never, she cried, never could she contemplate marriage with Mr. Mathews She esteemed him; she admired him; she thought him the first comic actor of the age; that was all. Charles himself fairly scolded the dying woman for putting them in such an awful predicament. He ran after the sobbing girl to implore her to believe that it was none of his doing—that his wife was raving and no longer knew what she said. And so Eliza died. For months a coldness, an awkwardness, existed between the widower and his wife's friend. They scarcely met. Then at the same moment on the same night the same vision visited them, far apart as they were, in their sleep. Eliza came imploring to the side of each. Well, said Anne, it must be destiny; Shakespeare said so; "marriage comes of destiny", he said, and she was disposed to agree with Shakespeare. Twelve months after she had sworn that she could never feel anything but esteem for Mr. Mathews, she was his wife.

But what conclusion are we led to draw from the behaviour of Sterne's ghost? Was it malicious or tender, did it come to warn or to mock, or merely to dip its handkerchief once more in the tears of lovers? Nobody could say. Charles Mathews told the story of the Stonegate ghost a hundred times in the green room at York, but nobody came forward with an explanation. Again one night he was telling the story, when an old actress who had returned to the stage after a long absence and had heard nothing of the ghost or of the Mathews, exclaimed in astonishment "Why, that was my dear Billy Leng!" And then she told them how they lodged next door to Mrs. Simpson's in Stonegate; how her dear Billy had been bedridden for many years; how, as his infirmities increased, so did his fear of robbers; how, being the most methodical of men, and growing more so with age, he waited always for York Minster to chime midnight and then took his crutch-handled stick and beat forcibly on the calico at the back of his bed to warn any thief who might be concealed there. "It was no ghost," she cried, "it was my dear Billy Leng!"

Cleared of the imputation which the ghost of Sterne had cast upon them, Mrs. Simpson now let her rooms for the ordinary sum.

Mrs. Thrale

No one can destroy Boswell's sketch of Mrs. Thrale. It is done with such venom and such vivacity; it contains so much of Boswell himself, and, like all Boswell's portraits, it fits so perfectly into its place in the picture. But Mr. Clifford [1] has done what is far more valuable and more difficult. He has gone behind Boswell's sketch and beyond it. He has amplified it and solidified it. He has brought Mrs. Thrale herself into the foreground. And by so doing he has changed the proportions of the picture.

Mrs. Thrale herself has lived an ambiguous scattered life all these years in a mass of half published or unpublished documents sprinkled over England and America. And for years Mr. Clifford has been tracking her down and piecing her together with the most devoted care and the most triumphant results. If it were not that her diary and her commonplace book are still in the hands of an American editor, we should suppose that the whole woman is now before us. As it is we know her better perhaps than almost any living person. We can follow her, as we cannot follow our friends, at a foot's pace for more than eighty years. Yet the effect of this minute illumination is baffling. The more we know of people the less we can sum them up. Just as we think to hold the bird in our hands, the bird flits off. Who can explain, for example, why the brilliant and precocious Hester consented to marry the man whom Mr. Clifford now reveals in his entirety—the odious Thrale? When her father discovered their clandestine correspondence he fell dead in a fit. And for once the incompetent, irascible, impecunious Welsh squire was in the right. No marriage could have been more incongruous. Hester was impressionable, generous, intellectual. Thrale was a cold, callous, conventional man of business who aped the habits of the aristocracy but was

Written in February 1941
[1] *Hester Lynch Piozzi (Mrs. Thrale)*. By James L. Clifford.

45

without their distinction, who had the grossness of the middle class but lacked their geniality. If he had any affection besides his passion for meat and drink, it was not for Hester but for her mother. Yet Hester married him and was at once immured in the great house at Streatham, "like a kept mistress", as Johnson said, "shut from the world".

It was her marriage, however, that gave depth to her relationship with Johnson. Had she been happy, she would never have known him as she did. He gave her, of course, the obvious things—stimulus, society, an outlet for her irrepressible curiosity and ambition. But the friendship between the young wife and the old man was based on deeper things. Johnson was not merely a distinguished guest at dinner. He had the run of the house. He and his hostess went together behind the scenes. It was to Johnson that Mrs. Thrale turned when her eyes were red with crying—when Queeney snubbed her; when Mr. Thrale took another mistress; when ruin threatened them; when one after another the children were born, and the children fell ill and died. "What shall I do? What can I do? Has the flattery of my friends made me too proud of my Brains? and must these poor Children suffer for my crime?" she cried out to him in her anguish. He gave her counsel and confidence. In return she gave him a share in the family, a stake in the next generation, and domesticity. It was by "the pump-side in the kitchen garden" at Streatham that Johnson was caught "fusing metals" when Mr. Thrale came back from the city and put out the fire. One anecdote sums up their relationship. Johnson had been more than usually rude to her in company, and some one protested. But Mrs. Thrale passed it off with a smile. "Oh dear good man!" she said. And when the words were repeated to Johnson "he seemed much delighted . . . and repeated in a loud whisper, Oh dear good man!"

Why, then, when Mr. Thrale finally ate himself to death, did a friendship that had been daily rubbed and tried for sixteen years come to an end? Partly, as Mr. Clifford makes plain, because Mrs. Thrale had suppressed a great deal. She had certain individual tastes of her own. One was a romantic passion for the scenery of Wales; another was a genuine love for painting. But when the three of them travelled in Wales,

neither Johnson nor Thrale had a word of praise for the landscape; and in Paris she was left to gaze for hours in the galleries
alone. Again as a writer—she scribbled incessantly—she was by
nature an innovator. "Why, she wondered, should there be one
set of words for writing and another for speaking?" She saw no
reason why one should not write as one speaks, familiarly,
colloquially; and her pages, "crowded with familiar phrases
and vulgar idioms", roused the disgust of the conventional.
Clearly there were a thousand curiosities and desires dormant
in her that the old man could not gratify. So long as she was
Thrale's wife and the mistress of Streatham she must suppress
them. But when her husband's dead weight was lifted off her,
up she sprang. She became again the precocious and impulsive
Hester Salusbury. Perhaps marriage had kept her youth green
in her—she was only just past forty when she became a widow.
And one day before Thrale's death Mrs. Byron had warned
her, while Piozzi sang to the harpsichord: "You know, I suppose, that that man is in Love with you?"

"That man" is one of Mr. Clifford's most remarkable recon-
structions. To the Streatham circle he was merely "an Italian
musick master". When they had said that they had said
enough. But in fact he was an Italian gentleman of great charm
and cultivation; a composer and performer of merit; and a
passionate lover of music. He travelled with a small harpsichord fitted under the seat so that he could play Mozart and
Haydn on the roads. They floated on a barge down the Brenta
to the strains of his music. Nor was he lacking in the sober
virtues. He managed Mrs. Piozzi's tangled money matters
admirably, and he ended his days in Wales giving plum puddings to villagers and performing the duties of a country gentleman. Yet at the notion that such a man could marry a brewer's
widow, the whole company of distinguished people who had
feasted at her table took flight in one flock. Johnson trumpeted
his rage. "She has now become a subject for her enemies to
exult over, and for her friends, if she has any left, to forget or
pity." "Heaven be praised," exclaimed the Queen of the Blues,
"that I have no daughters." It was only charity that led her to
conclude that Mrs. Thrale was mad. For Johnson there is the
excuse that he had lost at one blow Streatham and its peaches

and its pork pies and the undivided attention of his lady. The old elephant was jealous, and his rage has at least the dignity of wounded passion. But how are we to explain the conduct of the others? Only perhaps by supposing that it is almost impossible even for genius and learning to swim against the conventions of their time. And while genius and learning come down the stream untouched, the conventions in which they exist soon become obsolete and ridiculous. An Italian music master in the eighteenth century was, we must suppose, equal to a negro to-day. To explain the conduct of the Streatham set we must imagine the attitude of society to-day to a lady of rank who has contracted an alliance with a negro and expects Mayfair to open its doors to her dusky and illegitimate brood.

But the more we excuse the Streatham set, the more we must admire Mrs. Piozzi. Her passion for Piozzi made her for once concentrated and direct. There is a fine ring in her letter to Johnson.

> The birth of my second husband [she told him] is not meaner than that of my first; his sentiments are not meaner; his profession is not meaner . . . till you have changed your opinion of Mr. Piozzi let us converse no more.

With those words she should have vanished down the Brenta to the strains of Mozart. Unfortunately, Mr. Clifford has an inexhaustible supply of those little facts that reduce music to common speech. With Johnson it is plain that Mrs. Thrale had lost her centre. Now there was some screw loose. The whirligig spins faster and faster. She was for ever dipping and sampling, quarrelling and chattering. She was impulsive and impressionable, but she was also obtuse and tactless. Her children found her intolerable. Fanny Burney resented her patronage. She decked her little body in grebe skins and tiger shawls and flaxen wigs and many-coloured ribbons. She made a fool of herself with her adopted nephew, and let herself be cheated out of six thousand pounds to buy him a baronetcy. There was a coarseness in her fibre and a commonness in her vision that explain why, as an observer, she was so greatly inferior to Boswell.

Yet the spin of the whirligig has its fascination. Her appetite for life was prodigious. She must have someone to worship.

Mrs. Siddons succeeded Dr. Johnson. Mr. Conway succeeded Mrs. Siddons. When there was no hero to entertain, she devoured books. And when the books were read, and the letters written, and the copy books filled, she had out her telescope and scoured the horizon. One day she counted forty-one sails out to sea. Then, turning her telescope to the earth, she discovered Sir John Williams five miles away searching for something in his garden. What could it be? She could not rest until she had sent a servant to ascertain that Sir John was looking for his watch.

At last, at the age of eighty, she led the dance at her birthday party with her nephew; and danced indefatigably till dawn. That was in 1820. By that time one has almost forgotten Boswell's sketch. It was a snapshot at one particular moment. But the moment has long been covered over. She has loved; she has travelled; she has known everybody; she has been in the depths of despair and on the crest of the wave times without counting. The portrait of the old lady in the huge bonnet shows a very modern face, with her great vivacious eyes, her loose lips, and the deep scar over the mouth which, by her own wish, the artist has faithfully depicted. For that was the scar she got when her horse threw her in 1774 at Streatham.

Sir Walter Scott

I. GAS AT ABBOTSFORD

Either Scott the novelist is swallowed whole and becomes part of the body and brain, or he is rejected entirely. There is no middle party in existence—no busybodies run from camp to camp with offers of mediation. For there is no war. The novels of Dickens, Trollope, Henry James, Tolstoy, the Brontës —they are discussed perpetually; the Waverley novels never. There they remain, completely accepted, entirely rejected— a queer stage in that ever-changing process which is called immortality. If anything is going to break the deadlock perhaps it is the first volume of Scott's Journal, 1825–1826, which Mr. J. G. Tait has been at immense pains to edit and revise. As Scott's Journals are the best life of Scott in existence, as they contain Scott in his glory and Scott in his gloom, and gossip about Byron, and the famous comment upon Jane Austen, as in a few passages Scott throws more light upon his genius and its limitations than all his critics in their innumerable volumes, this new version may one of these dark nights bring the two non-combatants to blows.

By way of inducing that desirable encounter, let us take the entry for November 21st, 1825: "Went to the Oil Gas Committee this morning, of which concern I am President or Chairman". Scott, as Lockhart tells us and we can well believe, had a passion for gas. He loved a bright light, and he did not mind a slight smell. As for the expense of those innumerable pipes, in dining-room, drawing-room, corridors, and bedrooms, and the men's wages—he swept all that aside in those glorious days when his imagination was at its height. "The state of an illumination was constantly kept up"; and the gas shone upon a brilliant company. Everyone was flocking to Abbotsford— dukes and duchesses, lion hunters and toadies, the famous and

Written in January 1940

the obscure. "Oh dear," Miss Scott exclaimed. "Will this never end, Papa?" And her father replied, "Let them come, the more the merrier." And someone else walked in.

One night, a year or two before the diary begins, the stranger was a young artist. Artists were so common at Abbotsford that Scott's dog, Maida, recognised them at sight and got up and left the room. This time it was William Bewick, obscure, penniless, in pursuit of sitters. Naturally he was a good deal dazzled both by the gas and the company. Kind Mrs. Hughes, therefore, the wife of the deaf Dean of St. Paul's, tried to put him at his ease. She told him how she had often soothed her children's quarrels by showing them Bewick's woodcuts. But William Bewick was no relation of Thomas Bewick. One feels that he had heard the remark before and rather resented it, for was he not a painter himself?

He was a painter himself, and an extremely bad one. Did not Haydon say "Bewick, my pupil, has realised my hopes in his picture of Jacob and Rachel"? Did he not add, some years later, when they had quarrelled about money, "Daniel's left foot and leg would have disgraced Bewick before he ran away from my tuition to the shelter of Academical wings"? But we know without Haydon's testimony that Bewick's portraits were intolerable. We know that from his writing. His friends are always painted in a state of violent physical agitation, but mentally they are stock still, stone dead. There is his picture of Hazlitt playing tennis. "He looked more like a savage animal than anything human. . . ." He cast off his shirt; he leapt; he darted; when the game was over he rubbed himself against a post, dripping with sweat. But when he spoke, "His ejaculations were interlarded", Bewick says, "with unintentional and unmeaning oaths." They cannot be repeated; they must be imagined; in other words, Hazlitt was dumb. Or take Bewick's account of an evening party in a small room when the Italian poet Foscolo met Wordsworth. They argued. Foscolo "deliberately doubled his fist and held it in Wordsworth's face close to his nose". Then, suddenly, he began whirling round the room, tossing his quizzing glass, rolling his R's, bawling. The ladies "drew in their feet and costumes". Wordsworth sat "opening his mouth and eyes, gasping for breath". At last he spoke. For

51

page after page he spoke; or rather dead phrases coagulated upon his lips, in frozen and lifeless entanglements. Listen for a moment. "Although I appreciate, and I hope, can admire sufficiently the beauties of Raphael's transcendent genius . . . yet we must brace the sinews, so to speak, of our comprehension to grapple with the grandeur and sublimity . . . of Michael Angelo. . . ." It is enough. We see Bewick's pictures; we realise how intolerable it became to sit any longer under the portrait of Grandpapa flinging out a bare arm from the toga while the horse in the background champs his bit, paws the ground, and seems to neigh.

That night at Abbotsford the gas blazed from the three great chandeliers over the dinner-table; and the dinner, "as my friend, Thackeray, would have said, was recherché". Then they went into the drawing-room—a vast apartment with its mirrors, its marble tables, Chantrey's bust, the varnished wood-work and the crimson tasselled curtains pendant from hand-some brass rods. They went in and Bewick was dazzled—"The brilliant gaslight, the elegance and taste displayed throughout this beautiful apartment, the costumes of the ladies, with the sparkle and glitter of the tea-table"—the scene, as Bewick describes it, brings back all the worst passages in the Waverley Novels. We can see the jewels sparkling, we can smell the gas escaping, we can hear the conversation. There is Lady Scott gossiping with kind Mrs. Hughes; there is Scott himself, prosing and pompous, grumbling about his son Charles and his passion for sport. "But I suppose it will have an end at a given time, like any other hobby of youth." To complete the horror, the German Baron D'este strums on the guitar. He is showing "how in Germany they introduced into guitar performances of martial music the imitation of the beating of drums". Miss Scott—or is she Miss Wardour or another of the vapid and vacant Waverley novel heroines?—hangs over him entranced. Then, suddenly, the whole scene changes. Scott began in a low mournful voice to recite the ballad of Sir Patrick Spens:

> Oh lang lang may their ladies sit
>   With their fans in their hands
> Or e'er they see Sir Patrick Spens
>   Come sailing to the land.

The guitar stopped; Sir Walter's lips trembled as he came to an end. So it happens, too, in the novels—the lifeless English turns to living Scots.

Bewick came again. Again he joined that extraordinary company, all distinguished either for their genius or for their rank. Again the tiny red beads of light in the chandeliers blossomed at the turn of a screw into "a gush of splendour worthy of the palace of Aladdin". And there they all were, those gas-lit celebrities, dashed in with the usual dabs of bright oily paint: Lord Minto in plain black, wearing a most primitive tie; Lord Minto's chaplain, with his saturnine expression and his hair combed and cut as if by the edge of a barber's basin; Lord Minto's servant, so enthralled by Scott's stories that he forgot to change the plates; Sir John Malcolm wearing his star and ribbon; and little Johnny Lockhart gazing at the star. "You must try and get hold of one," said Sir Walter, upon which Lockhart smiled, ". . . the only time I have observed him to relieve his fixed features from that impenetrable reserve, etc., etc." And again they went into that beautiful apartment, and Sir John announced that he was about to tell his famous Persian story. Everybody must be summoned. Summoned they were.

From all quarters of that teeming and hospitable house guests came flocking. "One young lady, I remember, was brought from her sick-bed wrapt in blankets and laid on the sofa." The story began; the story went on. So long was it that it had to be cut into "miles". At the end of one Sir John stopped and asked "Shall I go on?" "Do go on, do go on, Sir John," Lady Scott entreated, and on he went, mile after mile, until—from where?—there appeared Monsieur Alexandre, the French ventriloquist, who at once began to imitate the planing of a French-polished dinner-table. "The attitude, the action, the noise, the screeches and hitches at knots, throwing off the shavings with his left hand, were all so perfect that Lady Scott, in alarm, screamed 'Oh! my dining-room table, you are spoiling my dining-room table! It will never be got bright again!' " And Sir Walter had to reassure her. "It is only imitation, my dear . . . it is only make-believe . . . he will not hurt the table." And the screeching began again, and Lady Scott screamed again, and on it went, the screeching and the screaming, until

53

the sweat poured from the ventriloquist's forehead, and it was time for bed.

Scott took Bewick to his room; on the way he stopped; he spoke. His words were simple—oddly simple, and yet after all that gas and glitter they seem to come from the living lips of an ordinary human being. The muscles are relaxed; the toga slips off him. "You, I suppose, would be of the stock of Sir Robert Bewick?" That was all, but it was enough—enough to make Bewick feel that the great man, for all his greatness, had noted his discomfiture when Mrs. Hughes was so tactful, and wished to give him his chance. He took it. "I," he exclaimed, "am of a very ancient family, the Bewicks of Annan, who lost their estates . . ." Out it all came; on it all went. Then Scott opened the bedroom door, and showed him the gas—how you can turn it up, how you can turn it down. And, expressing the hope that his guest would be comfortable—if not, he was to ring the bell—Scott left him. But Bewick could not sleep. He tossed and tumbled. He thought, as the people in his pictures must have thought, about magicians' cells, alchemists' spells, lions' lairs, the pallet of poverty, and the downy couch of luxury. Then, remembering the great man and his goodness, he burst into tears, prayed, and fell asleep.

We, however, can follow Scott to his room. By the light of his journals, the natural and fitful light of happiness and sorrow, we can see him after the party was over, when poor Charlotte chattered no more, and Maida had gone where, let us hope, artists no longer paint the favourite dogs of celebrated men. But after a party is over, some saying, some figure often remains in the mind. Now it is the ventriloquist, Monsieur Alexandre. Was Scott himself, we ask, glancing at the long line of the Waverley Novels, merely the greatest of all the ventriloquist novelists, of all who imitate human speech without hurting the dining-room table—it is all make-believe, my dear, it is all imitation? Or was he the last of the playwright novelists, who, when the pressure of emotion is strong enough behind them can leap the bounds of prose and make real thoughts and real emotions issue in real words from living lips? So many playwrights did; but of novelists who—except Sir Walter and, perhaps, Dickens? To write as they did, to keep so hospitable and teeming a house, where earls and artists, ventriloquists and barons, dogs and young ladies speak each in character, must not one be as they were, half-ventriloquist, half-poet? And is it not the combination in the Waverley Novels of gas and daylight, ventriloquy and truth, that separates the two parties, and might they not, using the journals as stepping-stones, with a glance at these crude illustrations from the brush of William Bewick, break the deadlock and come to blows?

II. *THE ANTIQUARY*

THERE are some writers who have entirely ceased to influence others, whose fame is for that reason both serene and cloudless, who are enjoyed or neglected rather than criticised and read. Among them is Scott. The most impressionable beginner, whose pen oscillates if exposed within a mile of the influence of Stendhal, Flaubert, Henry James, or Chekhov, can read the Waverley Novels one after another without altering an adjective. Yet there are no books perhaps upon which at this moment more thousands of readers are brooding and feasting in a rapture of uncritical and silent satisfaction. And if this is the mood in which the Waverley Novels are read, the inference is perhaps that there is something vicious about such a pleasure; it cannot be defended; it must be enjoyed in secret. Let us run through *The Antiquary* again and make a note or two as we go. The first charge that is levelled against Scott is that his style is execrable. Every page of the novel, it is true, is watered down with long languid Latin words—peruse, manifest, evince. Old metaphors out of the property box come flapping their dusty wings across the sky. The sea in the heat of a crisis is "the devouring element". A gull on the same occasion is a "winged denizen of the crag". Taken from their context it is impossible to deny that such expressions sound wrong, though a good case might be made against the snobbery which insists upon preserving class distinctions even among words. But read currently

Written in 1924

in their places, it is difficult either to notice or to condemn them. As Scott uses them they fulfil their purpose and merge perfectly in their surroundings. Great novelists who are going to fill seventy volumes write after all in pages, not in sentences, and have at their command, and know when to use, a dozen different styles of varying intensities. The genteel pen is a very useful pen in its place. These slips and slovenlinesses serve as relaxations; they give the reader breathing space and air the book. Let us compare Scott the slovenly with Stevenson the precise. "It was as he said: there was not a breath stirring; a windless stricture of frost had bound the air; and as we went forth in the shine of the candles, the blackness was like a roof over our heads." One may search the Waverley Novels in vain for such close writing as this. But if we get from Stevenson a much closer idea of a single object, we get from Scott an incomparably larger impression of the whole. The storm in *The Antiquary*, made up as it is of stage hangings and cardboard screens, of "denizens of the crags" and "clouds like disasters round a sinking empire", nevertheless roars and splashes and almost devours the group huddled on the crag; while the storm in *Kidnapped*, for all its exact detail and its neat dapper adjectives, is incapable of wetting the sole of a lady's slipper.

The much more serious charge against Scott is that he used the wrong pen, the genteel pen, not merely to fill in the background and dash off a cloud piece, but to describe the intricacies and passions of the human heart. But what language to use of the Lovels and Isabellas, the Darsies, Ediths, and Mortons! As well talk of the hearts of seagulls and the passions and intricacies of walking-sticks and umbrellas; for indeed these ladies and gentlemen are scarcely to be distinguished from the winged denizens of the crag. They are equally futile; equally impotent; they squeak; they flutter; and a strong smell of camphor exudes from their poor dried breasts when, with a dismal croaking and cawing, they emit the astonishing language of their love-making.

"Without my father's consent, I will never entertain the addresses of anyone; and how totally impossible it is that he should countenance the partiality with which you honour me, you are yourself fully aware," says the young lady. "Do not add to the severity of repelling my sentiments the rigour of obliging me to disavow them," replies the young gentleman; and he may be illegitimate, and he may be the son of a peer, or he may be both one and the other, but it would take a far stronger inducement than that to make us care a straw what happens to Lovel and his Isabella.

But then, perhaps, we are not meant to care a straw. When Scott has pacified his conscience as a magistrate by alluding to the sentiments of the upper classes in tones of respect and esteem, when he has vindicated his character as a moralist by awakening "the better feelings and sympathies of his readers by strains of generous sentiment and tales of fictitious woe", he was quit both of art and of morals, and could scribble endlessly for his own amusement. Never was a change more emphatic; never one more wholly to the good. One is tempted, indeed, to suppose that he did it, half-consciously, on purpose—he showed up the languor of the fine gentlemen who bored him by the immense vivacity of the common people whom he loved. Images, anecdotes, illustrations drawn from sea, sky, and earth, race and bubble from their lips. They shoot every thought as it flies, and bring it tumbling to the ground in metaphor. Sometimes it is a phrase—"at the back of a dyke, in a wreath o' snaw, or in the wame o' a wave"; sometimes a proverb—"he'll no can haud down his head to sneeze, for fear o' seeing his shoon"; always the dialogue is sharpened and pointed by the use of that Scottish dialect which is at once so homely and so pungent, so colloquial and so passionate, so shrewd and so melancholy into the bargain. And the result is strange. For since the sovereigns who should preside have abdicated, since we are afloat on a broad and breezy sea without a pilot, the Waverley Novels are as unmoral as Shakespeare's plays. Nor, for some readers, is it the least part of their astonishing freshness, their perennial vitality, that you may read them over and over again, and never know for certain what Scott himself was or what Scott himself thought.

We know, however, what his characters are, and we know it almost as we know what our friends are by hearing their voices and watching their faces simultaneously. However often one may have read *The Antiquary*, Jonathan Oldbuck is slightly different every time. We notice different things; our observation of face and voice differs; and thus Scott's characters, like Shakespeare's and Jane Austen's, have the seed of life in them. They change as we change. But though this gift is an essential element in what we call immortality, it does not by any means prove that the character lives as profoundly, as fully, as Falstaff lives or Hamlet. Scott's characters, indeed, suffer from a serious disability; it is only when they speak that they are alive; they never think; as for prying into their minds himself, or drawing inferences from their behaviour, Scott never attempted it. "Miss Wardour, as if she felt that she had said too much, turned and got into the carriage"—he will penetrate no further into the privacy of Miss Wardour than that; and it is not far. But this matters the less because the characters he cared for were by temperament chatterboxes; Edie Ochiltree, Oldbuck, Mrs. Mucklebackit talk incessantly. They reveal their characters in talk. If they stop talking it is to act. By their talk and by their acts—that is how we know them.

But how far then can we know people, the hostile critic may ask, if we only know that they say this and do that, if they never talk about themselves, and if their creator lets them go their ways, provided they forward his plot, in complete independence of his supervision or interference? Are they not all of them, Ochiltrees, Antiquaries, Dandy Dinmonts, and the rest, merely bundles of humours, and innocent childish humours at that, who serve to beguile our dull hours and charm our sick ones, and are packed off to the nursery when the working day returns and our normal faculties crave something tough to set their teeth into? Compare the Waverley Novels with the novels of Tolstoy, of Stendhal, of Proust! These comparisons of course lead to questions that lie at the root of fiction, but without discussing them, they reveal unmistakably what Scott is not. He is not among the great observers of the intricacies of the heart. He is not going to break seals or loose fountains. But he has the power of the artist who can create a scene and leave us to analyse it for ourselves. When we read the scene in the cottage where Steenie Mucklebackit lies dead, the different emotions— the father's grief, the mother's irritability, the minister's consolations—all rise spontaneously, as if Scott had merely to record, and we have merely to observe. What we lose in intricacy we gain perhaps in spontaneity and the stimulus given to our own creative powers. It is true that Scott creates carelessly, as if the parts came together without his willing it; it is true also that his scene breaks into ruin without his caring.

For who taps at the door and destroys that memorable scene? The cadaverous Earl of Glenallan; the unhappy nobleman who had married his sister in the belief that she was his cousin; and had stalked the world in sables ever after. Falsity breaks in; the peerage breaks in; all the trappings of the undertaker and heralds' office press upon us their unwholesome claims. The emotions then in which Scott excels are not those of human beings pitted against other human beings, but of man pitted against Nature, of man in relation to fate. His romance is the romance of hunted men hiding in woods at night; of brigs standing out to sea; of waves breaking in the moonlight; of solitary sands and distant horsemen; of violence and suspense. And he is perhaps the last novelist to practise the great, the Shakespearean art, of making people reveal themselves in speech.

Lockhart's Criticism

LOCKHART was not an ambitious man, and, for all his powers, he was, save in one instance, rather careless in the use he made of them. As a young man he was content with the irre- sponsibilities of anonymous reviewing; and as an older man the same ephemeral occupation suited him well enough, though he pursued it more sedately, less anonymously and from the respectable comfort of an editor's chair. But he held no very exalted view of his mission. The business of reviewers, he said, was "to think not of themselves, but of their author. . . . This excludes all chance of formal, original, or would-be original disquisition on the part of the journalist." Hence, though Lock- hart must have filled volume upon volume with his reviews, very little of Lockhart is to be found embedded in them. When his editor comes—armed with an admirable introduction—to pick out from the lumber of old *Blackwoods* and *Quarterlies* the true Lockhart himself, she finds, for all her enthusiasm, that one slim volume holds all that can now be saved.[1]

Yet the work was well worth doing, both because Lockhart had a bold, vivacious mind which leaked into his reviews in spite of his theories, and then again, though Miss Hildyard rates him too highly as a critic, he is a fine sample of a reviewer and serves to show the nature and function of those curious creatures whose lives, if they are as gay and giddy as a gnat's, are also as short. Here is one of them who has got himself, rather against his will, pinned down in a book; and it is highly amusing to look at him for a moment transfixed. His most necessary quality, it would seem, must be that which in other walks of life would be called, respectfully enough, courage. A new and unknown writer is a very dangerous person. Most of them die at a pinch without a gasp, but some survive and

Written in 1931
[1] *Lockhart's Literary Criticism.* With an Introduction and Biblio- graphy. By M. Clive Hildyard.

sting, and their sting can be fatal. When Lockhart, we have to
remember, saw ranged on his table the usual new books, their
names conveyed nothing to him. Keats, Hook, Godwin,
Shelley, Brontë, Tennyson—who were they? They might be
somebodies, but they might, more probably, be nobodies. It was
for him to make the trial and decide the question. Advancing
alone with nothing but his own judgment to support him,
the reviewer had need of all his courage, his acuteness, his
education. He had to switch as adroitly as he could from one
subject to another. Mr. Shelley and Mr. Keats, for example,
were both poets, and wrote about Greek myths. Godwin and
Brontë—Brontë might possibly be a woman—were both
novelists; Jeffrey was a critic; Macaulay an historian; Beckford
and Borrow were travellers; Coleridge was a poet again, but at
the same time a very different poet from Crabbe; somebody
had written a book about heraldry, a Staff surgeon had published his memoirs, General Nott had written about Afghanis-
tan, and there was also a valuable work about a new method
of treating dry rot. All had to be read, sorted, placed, marked
good or bad, and commended with a label tied round their
necks to the attention or neglect of the public. The public who
paid to be told what to read would be justly annoyed if they
were told to read the wrong things.

Lockhart was well qualified for the business. He was a highly
educated man. He had taken a first at Oxford, he had a considerable knowledge of Spanish literature, and he was more
widely read than most young men of his age. All this was in
his favour, but there were drawbacks. The Lockharts were an
old Scottish family; and when you add an Oxford education to
a young man of an old Scottish family you are making it very
difficult for him to be just to apothecaries, for example, who
think they can write poetry, or to Cockneys who have the
temerity to talk about the Greeks. Moreover, Lockhart was one
of those quick-witted indolent people who, as Sir Walter com-
plained, feel the attractions of "the gown and slipper garb of
life, and live with funny, easy companions" gossiping and telling stories instead of attending to the serious business of life
and making a name for themselves. The doors and windows of
his study let in rumours, prejudices, odds and ends of unsub-

stantiated gossip. With it all, however, he had the makings of a prince of reviewers; and those who have a kindly feeling for the race might well feel forebodings when he and his cronies picked up for review one day in 1820 a new book of poems by John Keats. Keats, Lockhart knew, was a friend of Leigh Hunt, and therefore presumably a Liberal, a Cockney. He knew vaguely that his father had kept livery stables. It was impossible, then, that he should be a gentleman and a scholar. All Lockhart's prejudices were roused and he rushed to his doom—the worst that can befall a reviewer. He committed himself violently, he betrayed himself completely. He tried to snuff out between finger and thumb one of the immortal lights of English literature. For that failure he has been gibbeted ever since. No one who sees him swinging in the wind can help a shudder and a sigh lest the same fate may one of these days be his. After all, new books of poems still appear.

And it is plain, as we turn over the pages of Lockhart's resurrected reviews, that to write about a new book the moment it comes out is a very different matter from writing about it fifty years afterwards. A new book is attached to life by a thousand minute filaments. Life goes on and the filaments break and disappear. But at the moment they ring and resound and set up all kinds of irrelevant responses. Keats was an apothecary and lived in Hampstead, and consorted with Leigh Hunt and the Cockneys: Shelley was an atheist and had irregular views upon marriage; the author of *Jane Eyre* might be a woman, and, if so, was a very coarse one. It is easy to say that these were ephemeral accidents and that Lockhart should have brushed them aside; but they rang loud in his ears, and he could no more have disregarded them and the prejudices of his readers than he could have flung aside his blue dressing-gown and marched down Albemarle Street in a tweed cap and plus fours.

But even so, Lockhart was not so far out as might be expected; in other words, he was very often of the same opinion as we are. He saw the importance of Wordsworth and Coleridge; he welcomed Borrow and Beckford; he placed *Jane Eyre*, in spite of its coarseness, very high. It is true that he predicted a long life for *Zohrab the Hostage*, who has had a short one. Probably because he was a novelist himself his criticism of fiction was erratic, and his enthusiasm for the novels of Godwin and Hook seems to show that they excited his own creative power and thus deflected his critical judgment. Tennyson he bullied with unchastened insolence, but, as Tennyson proved by accepting some of his criticism, not without acuteness. In short, the case of Lockhart would seem to show that a good reviewer of contemporary work will get the proportions roughly right, but the detail wrong. He will single out from a number of unknown writers those who are going to prove men of substance, but he cannot be certain what qualities are theirs in particular, or how the importance of one compares with the importance of another.

One may regret, since this is so, that Lockhart fixed his mind so much upon contemporaries and did not give himself the benefit of a wider perspective. He might have written with far greater safety and perhaps with far greater authority upon the dead. But he was a diffident man and a fastidious; and he knew that criticism, to be worth anything, requires more effort and more austerity than he was able to command. All the brilliance of Jeffrey, as he perceived, was not enough "to induce a man of research in the next century to turn over the volumes of his review". And Gifford, with his "illnatured abuse and cold rancorous raillery . . . is exquisitely formed for the purposes of political objurgation, but not at all for those of gentle and universal criticism". A reviewer can skim the surface, but there are "matters of such moment, that it is absolutely impossible to be a great critic while the mind remains unsettled in regard to them". Because he was aware of this, Lockhart was a good reviewer, and content to remain one. But he was too sceptical too diffident, too handsome and well bred perhaps; he lived too much under the shadow of Sir Walter Scott, he had too many worries and sorrows and dined out too often to push on into those calm and austere regions where the mind settles down to think things out and has its dwelling in a mood of gentle and universal contemplation. So he was content to go on knocking off articles, and cutting out quotations and leaving them to moulder where they lay. But if his reviews show by their power, their insolence, their very lack of ambition, that he had it in him to do better, they also remind us that there is a virtue in familiarity. We lose something when we have ceased to be able to talk naturally of Johnny Keats, to regret the "early death of this unfortunate and misguided gentleman" Mr. Shelley. A little of the irreverence with which Lockhart treated the living would do no harm to our more sober estimates of the dead.

David Copperfield

LIKE the ripening of strawberries, the swelling of apples, and all other natural processes, new editions of Dickens—cheap, pleasant-looking, well printed—are born into the world and call for no more notice than the season's plums and strawberries, save when by some chance the emergence of one of these masterpieces in its fresh green binding suggests an odd and overwhelming enterprise—that one should read *David Copperfield* for the second time. There is perhaps no person living who can remember reading *David Copperfield* for the first time. Like *Robinson Crusoe* and *Grimm's Fairy Tales* and the Waverley Novels, *Pickwick* and *David Copperfield* are not books, but stories communicated by word of mouth in those tender years when fact and fiction merge, and thus belong to the memories and myths of life, and not to its aesthetic experience. When we lift it from this hazy atmosphere, when we consider it as a book, bound and printed and ordered by the rules of art, what impression does *David Copperfield* make upon us? As Peggotty and Barkis, the rooks and the workbox with the picture of St. Paul's, Traddles who drew skeletons, the donkeys who would cross the green, Mr. Dick and the Memorial, Betsey Trotwood and Jip and Dora and Agnes and the Heeps and the Micawbers once more come to life with all their appurtenances and peculiarities, are they still possessed of the old fascination or have they in the interval been attacked by that parching wind which blows about books and, without our reading them, remodels them and changes their features while we sleep? The rumour about Dickens is to the effect that his sentiment is disgusting and his style commonplace; that in reading him every refinement must be hidden and every sensibility kept under glass; but that with these precautions and reservations he is of course Shakespearean; like Scott, a born creator; like Balzac, prodigious in his fecundity; but, rumour

Written in 1925

adds, it is strange that while one reads Shakespeare and one reads Scott, the precise moment for reading Dickens seldom comes our way.

This last charge may be resolved into this—that he lacks charm and idiosyncrasy, is everybody's writer and no one's in particular, is an institution, a monument, a public thoroughfare trodden dusty by a million feet. It is based largely upon the fact that of all great writers Dickens is both the least personally charming and the least personally present in his books. No one has ever loved Dickens as he loves Shakespeare and Scott. Both in his life and in his work the impression that he makes is the same. He has to perfection the virtues conventionally ascribed to the male; he is self-assertive, self-reliant, self-assured; energetic in the extreme. His message, when he parts the veil of the story and steps forward in person, is plain and forcible; he preaches the value of "plain hardworking qualities", of punctuality, order, diligence, of doing what lies before one with all one's might. Agitated as he was by the most violent passions, ablaze with indignation, teeming with queer characters, unable to keep the dreams out of his head at night, nobody appears, as we read him, more free from the foibles and eccentricities and charms of genius. He comes before us, as one of his biographers described him, "like a prosperous sea captain", stalwart, weather-beaten, self-reliant, with a great contempt for the finicky, the inefficient, or the effeminate. His sympathies indeed have strict limitations. Speaking roughly, they fail him whenever a man or woman has more than two thousand a year, has been to the university, or can count his ancestors back to the third generation. They fail him when he has to treat of the mature emotions—the seduction of Emily, for example, or the death of Dora; whenever it is no longer possible to keep moving and creating, but it is necessary to stand still and search into things and penetrate to the depths of what is there. Then, indeed, he fails grotesquely, and the pages in which he describes what in our convention are the peaks and pinnacles of human life, the explanation of Mrs. Strong, the despair of Mrs. Steerforth, or the anguish of Ham, are of an indescribable unreality—of that uncomfortable complexion which, if we heard Dickens talking so in real life, would either make us blush to the roots of our hair or dash out of the room to conceal our laughter. ". . . Tell him then," says Emily, "that when I hear the wind blowing at night I feel as if it was passing angrily from seeing him and uncle, and was going up to God against me." Miss Dartle raves—about carrion and pollution and earthworms, and worthless spangles and broken toys, and how she will have Emily "proclaimed on the common stair". The failure is akin to that other failure to think deeply, to describe beautifully. Of the men who go to make up the perfect novelist and should live in amity under his hat, two—the poet and the philosopher—failed to come when Dickens called them.

But the greater the creator the more derelict the regions where his powers fail him; all about their fertile lands are deserts where not a blade of grass grows, swamps where the foot sinks deep in mud. Nevertheless, while we are under their spell these great geniuses make us see the world any shape they choose. We remodel our psychological geography when we read Dickens; we forget that we have ever felt the delights of solitude or observed with wonder the intricate emotions of our friends, or luxuriated in the beauty of nature. What we remember is the ardour, the excitement, the humour, the oddity of people's characters; the smell and savour and soot of London; the incredible coincidences which hook the most remote lives together; the city, the law courts; this man's nose, that man's limp; some scene under an archway or on the high road; and above all some gigantic and dominating figure, so stuffed and swollen with life that he does not exist singly and solitarily, but seems to need for his own realisation a host of others, to call into existence the severed parts that complete him, so that wherever he goes he is the centre of conviviality and merriment and punch-making; the room is full, the lights are bright; there are Mrs. Micawber, the twins, Traddles, Betsey Trotwood—all in full swing.

This is the power which cannot fade or fail in its effect—the power not to analyse or to interpret, but to produce, apparently without thought or effort or calculation of the effect upon the story, characters who exist not in detail, not accurately or exactly, but abundantly in a cluster of wild and yet extraordinarily revealing remarks, bubble climbing on the top of bubble as the breath of the creator fills them. And the fecundity and apparent irreflectiveness have a strange effect. They make creators of us, and not merely readers and spectators. As we listen to Micawber pouring himself forth and venturing perpetually some new flight of astonishing imagination, we see, unknown to Mr. Micawber, into the depths of his soul. We say, as Dickens himself says while Micawber holds forth: "How wonderfully like Mr. Micawber that is!" Why trouble, then, if the scenes where emotion and psychology are to be expected fail us completely? Subtlety and complexity are all there if we know where to look for them, if we can get over the surprise of finding them—as it seems to us, who have another convention in these matters—in the wrong places. As a creator of character his peculiarity is that he creates wherever his eyes rest—he has the visualising power in the extreme. His people are branded upon our eyeballs before we hear them speak, by what he sees them doing, and it seems as if it were the sight that sets his thought in action. He saw Uriah Heep "breathing into the pony's nostrils and immediately covering them with his hand"; he saw David Copperfield looking in the glass to see how red his eyes were after his mother's death; he saw oddities and blemishes, gestures and incidents, scars, eyebrows, everything that was in the room, in a second. His eye brings in almost too rich a harvest for him to deal with, and gives him an aloofness and a hardness which freeze his sentimentalism and make it seem a concession to the public, a veil thrown over the penetrating glance which left to itself pierced to the bone. With such a power at his command Dickens made his books blaze up, not by tightening the plot or sharpening the wit, but by throwing another handful of people upon the fire. The interest flags and he creates Miss Mowcher, completely alive, equipped in every detail as if she were to play a great part in the story, whereas once the dull stretch of road is passed by her help, she disappears; she is needed no longer. Hence a Dickens novel is apt to become a bunch of separate characters loosely held together, often by the most arbitrary conventions, who tend to fly asunder and split our attention into so many different parts that we drop the book in despair. But that danger is surmounted in *David Copperfield*. There, though characters swarm and life flows into every creek and cranny, some common feeling—youth, gaiety, hope—envelops the tumult, brings the scattered parts together, and invests the most perfect of all the Dickens novels with an atmosphere of beauty.[1]

[1] The following letter by Virginia Woolf appears in *The Nation* of September 12, 1925.

SIR,

Fear of a sudden death very naturally distracted Kappa's mind from my article on *David Copperfield* or he would, I think, have taken my meaning. That nobody can remember reading *David Copperfield* for the first time is a proof not, as he infers, that the reading makes so little impression that it slips off the mind unremembered, but that *David Copperfield* takes such rank among our classics and is a book of such astonishing vividness that parents will read it aloud to their children before they can quite distinguish fact from fiction, and they will never in later life be able to recall the first time they read it. *Grimm's Fairy Tales* and *Robinson Crusoe* are for many people in the same case.

Questions of affection are of course always disputable. I can only reiterate that while I would cheerfully become Shakespeare's cat, Scott's pig, or Keats's canary, if by so doing I could share the society of these great men, I would not cross the road (reasons of curiosity apart) to dine with Wordsworth, Byron, or Dickens. Yet I venerate their genius; and my tears would certainly help to swell the " unparalleled flow of popular grief" at their deaths. It only means that writers have characters apart from their books, which are sympathetic to some, antipathetic to others. And I maintain that if it could be put to the vote, Which do you prefer as man, Shakespeare, Scott, or Dickens? Shakespeare would be first, Scott second, and Dickens nowhere at all.

Yours, etc.,

VIRGINIA WOOLF

Lewis Carroll

THE complete works of Lewis Carroll have been issued by the Nonesuch Press in a stout volume of 1293 pages. So there is no excuse—Lewis Carroll ought once and for all to be complete. We ought to be able to grasp him whole and entire. But we fail—once more we fail. We think we have caught Lewis Carroll; we look again and see an Oxford clergyman. We think we have caught the Rev. C. L. Dodgson—we look again and see a fairy elf. The book breaks in two in our hands. In order to cement it, we turn to the Life.

But the Rev. C. L. Dodgson had no life. He passed through the world so lightly that he left no print. He melted so passively into Oxford that he is invisible. He accepted every convention; he was prudish, pernickety, pious, and jocose. If Oxford dons in the nineteenth century had an essence he was that essence. He was so good that his sisters worshipped him; so pure that his nephew has nothing to say about him. It is just possible, he hints, that "a shadow of disappointment lay over Lewis Carroll's life". Mr. Dodgson at once denies the shadow. "My life", he says, "is free from all trial and trouble." But this untinted jelly contained within it a perfectly hard crystal. It contained childhood. And this is very strange, for childhood normally fades slowly. Wisps of childhood persist when the boy or girl is a grown man or woman. Childhood returns sometimes by day, more often by night. But it was not so with Lewis Carroll. For some reason, we know not what, his childhood was sharply severed. It lodged in him whole and entire. He could not disperse it. And therefore as he grew older this impediment in the centre of his being, this hard block of pure childhood, starved the mature man of nourishment. He slipped through the grown-up world like a shadow, solidifying only on the beach at Eastbourne, with little girls whose frocks he pinned up with safety pins. But since childhood remained in him entire, he could do what no one else has ever been able to do—

Written in January 1939

70

he could return to that world; he could re-create it, so that we too become children again.

In order to make us into children, he first makes us asleep. "Down, down, down, would the fall *never* come to an end?" Down, down, down we fall into that terrifying, wildly inconsequent, yet perfectly logical world where time races, then stands still; where space stretches, then contracts. It is the world of sleep; it is also the world of dreams. Without any conscious effort dreams come; the white rabbit, the walrus, and the carpenter, one after another, turning and changing one into the other, they come skipping and leaping across the mind. It is for this reason that the two Alices are not books for children; they are the only books in which we become children. President Wilson, Queen Victoria, *The Times* leader writer, the late Lord Salisbury—it does not matter how old, how important, or how insignificant you are, you become a child again. To become a child is to be very literal; to find everything so strange that nothing is surprising; to be heartless, to be ruthless, yet to be so passionate that a snub or a shadow drapes the world in gloom. It is to be Alice in Wonderland.

It is also to be Alice Through the Looking Glass. It is to see the world upside down. Many great satirists and moralists have shown us the world upside down, and have made us see it, as grown-up people see it, savagely. Only Lewis Carroll has shown us the world upside down as a child sees it, and has made us laugh as children laugh, irresponsibly. Down the groves of pure nonsense we whirl laughing, laughing—

> *They sought it with thimbles, they sought it with care;*
> *They pursued it with forks and hope . . .*

And then we wake. None of the transitions in Alice in Wonderland is quite so queer. For we wake to find—is it the Rev. C. L. Dodgson? Is it Lewis Carroll? Or is it both combined? This conglomerate object intends to produce an extra-Bowdlerised edition of Shakespeare for the use of British maidens; implores them to think of death when they go to the play; and always, always to realise that "the true object of life is the development of *character*. . . ." Is there, then, even in 1293 pages, any such thing as "completeness"?

71

Edmund Gosse

WHEN famous writers die it is remarkable how frequently they are credited with one particular virtue—the virtue of kindness to the young and obscure. Every newspaper has lately contained that eulogy upon Arnold Bennett. And here is the same tribute paid to another writer who differed in every possible way from Arnold Bennett—Sir Edmund Gosse. He too, it is said, was generous to the young and obscure. Of Bennett it was certainly, although on some occasions rather obliquely, true. He might, that is to say, have formed a very low opinion of a book; he might have expressed that opinion as his habit was, bluntly and emphatically in print; and yet if he met the writer his sincerity, his concern, his assumption that both cared equally for the craft of letters made it perfectly easy for that unfortunate person to say, "It is all true, and more than true, Mr. Bennett; but if you hate my books, I can't tell you how completely I loathe yours"—after which a frank discussion of fiction and its nature was possible; and a very obscure novelist was left with the feeling that a very famous one was indeed the kindest of men.

But what would have happened if, taking advantage of Sir Edmund's generosity, and assuming a common respect for letters, one had said, "But you can't hate my books, Sir Edmund, more than I hate yours"? Instant annihilation would have been the only and the happiest solution of the situation. But nobody who had ever seen Sir Edmund in the flesh would have risked such folly. Bristling and brilliant, formal but uneasy, he radiated even from a distance all the susceptibilities that make young writers draw in their horns. Generous was not the adjective that sprang to the lips at the sight of him, nor is it one that frequently occurs on reading the life of him by Mr. Charteris. He could be as touchy as a housemaid and as suspicious as a governess. He could smell out an offence where none was meant, and hoard a grievance for years. He could

72

quarrel permanently because a lamp wick was snuffed out too vigorously at a table under his nose. Hostile reviews threw him into paroxysms of rage and despair. His letters are full of phrases like "Mr. Clement Shorter, in terms of unexampled insolence, speaks of me as 'the so-called critic'. . . . If that insolent notice in *The Times* is true . . . it is better I should know it. . . . I feel I shall never have the heart to write another sentence." It seems possible that one severe review by Churton Collins gave him more pain than he suffered from any private or public sorrow in the course of seventy-nine years. All this must have made him the most prickly of companions, and the young must have been possessed of greater tact than the young usually possess to reach the kindness that no doubt lay hid behind the thorns. For the great merit of the present biography is that it does not attempt to conceal the fact that Sir Edmund was a complex character composed of many different strains. Plain virtue was not a sure passport to his affection. He could disregard genius and ignore merit if they trod too clumsily upon his toes. On the other hand the House of Lords possessed a distinct glamour for him; the rigours of high society delighted him; and to see the words "Marlborough Club" at the head of his notepaper did, it seems, shed a certain lustre upon the page.

But these foibles, amusing and annoying as they are, become at once more interesting and less irritating when we learn that there lay behind them a very good cause—his education, his childhood. "Far more than might be supposed of his conduct in life", writes Mr. Charteris, "was due to unconscious protest against . . . the things which darkened his childhood." Readers of *Father and Son* know well what those things were—the narrowness, the ugliness of his upbringing; the almost insane religious mania of his father; the absence from his home of culture, beauty, urbanity, graciousness—in fact, of all those elements in life to which Edmund Gosse turned as instinctively and needed as profoundly as a flower the sun. What could be more natural than that the flower, once transplanted, should turn, almost violently, the other way, should climb too high, should twine too lavishly, should—to drop these metaphors—order clothes in Savile Row and emerge from behind the form of

Dr. Fog uttering what appear at this distance of time rather excessive praises of the now little known Danish poet, Paludin Müller?—a surly poet who objected to visitors. But young Edmund Gosse triumphed. "Slowly, the poet murmured, 'You flatter me too much, but thank you.' The most stubborn of all the citadels had capitulated."

Few people can have been pitchforked, as Mr. Charteris calls it, into the world by a more violent propulsion than that which Gosse was given by the bleakness of his upbringing. It was no wonder that he overshot the mark, never quite got his equilibrium at parties which he loved, required to know the maiden names of married guests, and observed formalities punctiliously which are taken as a matter of course by those who have never lived in dread of the instant coming of the Lord, and have ordered their clothes for generations in Savile Row. But the impulse itself was generous, and the tokens of kindling and expansion more admirable than ridiculous. The "sensual sufficiency in life" delighted one who had been starved of it. Happiness formed the staple of what he would certainly not have called his creed. "To feel so saturated with the love of things", to enjoy life and "suck it as a wasp drains a peach", to "roll the moments on one's tongue and keep the flavour of them"; above all, to cherish friendship and exalt the ideals of friendship—such were the enjoyments that his nature, long repressed, stretched out to, generously, naturally, spontaneously. And yet . . .

Those who are acquainted with Sir Edmund's lively portraits know what demure but devastating qualifications he was able to insinuate after those two small words. "He possessed the truth and answered to the heavenly calling," he wrote of Andrew Lang, "and yet. . . ." Such expansion was natural, was right, was creditable, and yet, we echo, how much better Gosse would have been as a writer, how much more important he would have been as a man if only he had given freer rein to his impulses, if only his pagan and sensual joy had not been dashed by perpetual caution! The peculiarity which Mr. Charteris notes in his walk—"curiously suggestive at once of eagerness and caution"—runs through his life and limits his intelligence. He hints, he qualifies, he insinuates, he suggests, but he never speaks out, for all the world as if some austere Plymouth Brother were lying in wait to make him do penance for his audacity. Yet it seems possible, given the nature of his gifts, that if only he had possessed greater boldness, if only he had pushed his curiosity further, had incurred wrath instead of irritation, and complete confusion instead of some petty social tribulation, he might have rivalled the great Boswell himself. When we read how young Edmund Gosse insinuated himself under cover of Dr. Fog into the presence of an irascible poet and won the day by the adroitness of his flattery, we are reminded of the methods of Boswell in pursuit of Paoli or Voltaire or Johnson. Both men were irresistibly attracted by genius. Both had "a medium-like" power of drawing other people's confidences into the open. Both were astonishingly adept at reporting the talk and describing the appearance of their friends. But where Boswell is drawn headlong by the momentum of his hero and his own veneration beyond discretion, beyond vanity, beyond his fear of what people will say, down into the depths, Gosse is kept by his respect for decorum, by his decency and his timidity dipping and ducking, fingering and faltering upon the surface. Thus where Boswell left us that profound and moving master-piece, the *Life of Johnson*, Gosse left us *Father and Son*, a classic doubtless, as Mr. Charteris claims, certainly a most original and entertaining book, but how little and light, how dapper and superficial Gosse's portraits appear if we compare them with the portraits left by Boswell himself! Fear seems always to dog his footsteps. He dips his fingers with astonishing agility and speed into character, but if he finds something hot or gets hold of something large, he drops it and withdraws with the agility of a scalded cat. Thus we never know his sitters inti-mately; we never plunge into the depths of their minds or into the more profound regions of their hearts. But we know all that can be known by someone who is always a little afraid of being found out.

But if Gosse's masterpiece and his portraits suffer from his innate regard for caution, much of the fault must be laid upon his age. Even the most superficial student of letters must be aware that in the nineteenth century literature had become, for one reason or another, a profession rather than a vocation, a married woman rather than a lady of easy virtue. It had its organisation, its functions, its emoluments, and a host of people, not primarily writers, were attached to its service. Among them Gosse, of course, was one of the most eminent. ". . . No public dinner where literature was involved", writes Mr. Charteris, "was complete without Gosse to propose or to return thanks for the cause." He welcomed strangers, addressed bodies, celebrated centenaries, presented prizes, and represented letters on all occasions and with the highest delight in the function. Then, again, some intellectual curiosity had risen in the nineties and ardent if uninstructed ladies wished to be enlightened. Here again Gosse was invaluable. By an odd irony, while Churton Collins, his deadly foe, was lecturing in St. James's Square, Gosse was serving up Matthew Arnold to "some of the smartest women in London" in Bruton Street. After this, says Mr. Charteris, he became "a much more frequent guest in Mayfair" and his appetite for social life was whetted. Nothing would be more foolish than to sneer at a natural love of ceremony or a natural respect for the aristocracy, and yet it seems possible that this concern with the ritual of literature, this scrupulous observance of the rites of society encouraged Edmund Gosse in his growing decorum. Friendship had been his ideal; nobody can question the warmth of his youthful affection for Hamo Thornycroft; and yet when one of his friends, Robert Ross, was involved in a famous scandal he could write "I miss your charming company in which I have always delighted . . . I would say to you—be calm, be reasonable, turn for consolation to the infinite resources of literature. . . . Write to me when you feel inclined, and however busy I am I will write in reply, and in a more happy season you must come back and be truly welcomed in this house." Is that the voice of friendship, disinterested, fearless, sincere, or the voice of an uneasy man of letters, who is terribly afraid that dear Lady C. will not ask him to dine, or that divine being the Countess of D. will not invite him for the week-end if they suspect him of harbouring Robert Ross, the friend of Oscar Wilde? And later his decorum seems to have drawn a film over his wonted perspicacity as a critic. M. Gide, for example, thought it well to mention certain facts openly in the third volume of his memoirs. "Was it wise? Was

it necessary? Is it useful?" Sir Edmund cried, in "painful perplexity". And he was terribly shocked by an incident in E. M.
Forster's *Howards End*. "I should like to know", he wrote to
Mr. Marsh, "what you think of the new craze for introducing
into fiction the high-born maiden who has had a baby? . . . I
do not know how an Englishman can calmly write of such a
disgusting thing, with such *sang-froid*. . . . I cannot help hoping
that you may be induced to say something that will redeem
him." But when Sir Edmund goes on to say that no high-bred
maiden has ever had a baby illegitimately in a French novel
one can only suppose that he was thinking, not unnaturally,
of the House of Lords.

But if Gosse was no Boswell and still less a St. Francis, he
was able to fill a place and create a legend, and perhaps we
have no right to demand more. To be oneself is, after all, an
achievement of some rarity, and Gosse, as everybody must
agree, achieved it, both in literature and in life. As a writer he
expressed himself in book after book of history, of biography,
of criticism. For over fifty years he was busily concerned, as he
put it, with "the literary character and the literary craft".
There is scarcely a figure of any distinction, or a book of any
importance in modern letters, upon which we cannot have
Gosse's opinion if we wish for it. For instance, one may have a
curiosity about Disraeli's novels and hesitate which to begin
upon. Let us consult Gosse. Gosse advises on the whole that
we shall try *Coningsby*. He gives his reasons. He rouses us with
a suggestive remark. He defines Disraeli's quality by comparing him with Bulwer, with Mrs. Gore and Plumer Read.
He tells an anecdote about Disraeli that was told him by his
friend the Duke of Rutland. He breaks off a phrase here and
there for our amusement or admiration. All this he does with
perfect suavity and precision, so that by the time he has done
Disraeli is left glowing and mantling like an old picture lit up
by a dozen bright candles. To illumine, to make visible and
desirable, was his aim as a critic. Literature to him was an
incomparable mistress and it was his delight "to dress her
charms and make her more beloved". Lovers of course sometimes go further and a child is the result. Critics too sometimes
love literature creatively and the fruit of their devotion has a

toughness and a fibre that the smooth strains of Sir Edmund's platonic devotion are entirely without. Like all critics who persist in judging without creating he forgets the risk and agony of child-birth. His criticism becomes more and more a criticism of the finished article, and not of the article in the making. The smoothness, the craftsmanship of the work rouse his appreciation and he directs our attention only to its more superficial aspects. In other words, he is a critic for those who read rather than for those who write. But then no creator possesses Gosse's impartiality, or his width of reading, or his lightness and freedom of mind, so that if we want to hold a candle to some dark face in the long portrait gallery of literature there is no better illuminant than Edmund Gosse.

As for his own face, his own idiosyncrasy, only those who saw him at home among his books, or heard him, mimicking, remembering, in one of those club corners that he made, so characteristically, his own, can bring the odds and ends of this excitable but timid, this enthusiastic but worldly, this kindly but spiteful man into one complete synthesis. It was only in talk that he completely expressed himself. "I was not born for solitude", he wrote. Neither was he born for old age and meditation. "You speak of 'the peace which the years bring', but they bring no peace for me", he wrote. Thought and the ardours and agonies of life were not for him. "I have no idea", he said, "how the spiritual world would look to me, for I have never glanced at it since I was a child and gorged with it." It is a cruel fate that makes those who only come into being when they talk fall silent. It is a harsh necessity that brings these warm and mobile characters into the narrow confines of the grave. Sir Edmund was not in the least anxious to depart and leave a world which, with the solitary exception of Churton Collins, had showered upon him so many delightful gifts for seventy-nine years.

Notes on D. H. Lawrence

THE partiality, the inevitable imperfection of contemporary criticism can best be guarded against, perhaps, by making in the first place a full confession of one's disabilities, so far as it is possible to distinguish them. Thus by way of preface to the following remarks upon D. H. Lawrence, the present writer has to state that until April 1931 he was known to her almost solely by reputation and scarcely at all by experience. His reputation, which was that of a prophet, the exponent of some mystical theory of sex, the devotee of cryptic terms, the inventor of a new terminology which made free use of such words as solar plexus and the like, was not attractive; to follow submissively in his tracks seemed an unthinkable aberration; and as chance would have it, the few pieces of his writing that issued from behind this dark cloud of reputation seemed unable to rouse any sharp curiosity or to dispel the lurid phantom. There was, to begin with, *Trespassers*, a hot, scented, overwrought piece of work, as it seemed; then *A Prussian Officer*, of which no clear impression remained except of starting muscles and forced obscenity; then *The Lost Girl*, a compact and seamanlike piece of work, stuffed with careful observation rather in the Bennett manner; then one or two sketches of Italian travel of great beauty, but fragmentary and broken off; and then two little books of poems, *Nettles* and *Pansies*, which read like the sayings that small boys scribble upon stiles to make housemaids jump and titter.

Meanwhile, the chants of the worshippers at the shrine of Lawrence became more rapt; their incense thicker and their gyrations more mazy and more mystic. His death last year gave them still greater liberty and still greater impetus; his death, too, irritated the respectable; and it was the irritation roused by the devout and the shocked, and the ceremonies of the devout and the scandal of the shocked, that drove one at last to read *Sons and Lovers* in order to see whether, as so often happens,

79

the master is not altogether different from the travesty presented by his disciples.

This then was the angle of approach, and it will be seen that
it is an angle that shuts off many views and distorts others. But
read from this angle, *Sons and Lovers* emerged with astonishing
vividness, like an island from off which the mist has suddenly
lifted. Here it lay, clean cut, decisive, masterly, hard as rock,
shaped, proportioned by a man who, whatever else he might
be—prophet or villain, was undoubtedly the son of a miner
who had been born and bred in Nottingham. But this hardness,
this clarity, this admirable economy and sharpness of the stroke
are not rare qualities in an age of highly efficient novelists. The
lucidity, the ease, the power of the writer to indicate with one
stroke and then to refrain indicated a mind of great power and
penetration. But these impressions, after they had built up the
lives of the Morels, their kitchens, food, sinks, manner of
speech, were succeeded by another far rarer, and of far greater
interest. For after we have exclaimed that this coloured and
stereoscopic representation of life is so like that surely it must
be alive—like the bird that pecked the cherry in the picture—
one feels, from some indescribable brilliance, sombreness,
significance, that the room is put into order. Some hand has
been at work before we entered. Casual and natural as the
arrangement seems, as if we had opened the door and come in
by chance, some hand, some eye of astonishing penetration and
force, has swiftly arranged the whole scene, so that we feel that
it is more exciting, more moving, in some ways fuller of life
than one had thought real life could be, as if a painter had
brought out the leaf or the tulip or the jar by pulling a green
curtain behind it. But what is the green curtain that Lawrence
has pulled so as to accentuate the colours? One never catches
Lawrence—this is one of his most remarkable qualities—
"arranging". Words, scenes flow as fast and direct as if he
merely traced them with a free rapid hand on sheet after sheet.
Not a sentence seems thought about twice: not a word added
for its effect on the architecture of the phrase. There is no
arrangement that makes us say: "Look at this. This scene, this
dialogue has the meaning of the book hidden in it." One of the
curious qualities of *Sons and Lovers* is that one feels an unrest, a

little quiver and shimmer in his page, as if it were composed of separate gleaming objects, by no means content to stand still and be looked at. There is a scene of course; a character; yes, and people related to each other by a net of sensations; but these are not there—as in Proust—for themselves. They do not admit of prolonged exploration, of rapture in them for the sake of rapture, as one may sit in front of the famous hawthorn hedge in *Swann's Way* and look at it. No, there is always something further on, another goal. The impatience, the need for getting on beyond the object before us, seem to contract, to shrivel up, to curtail scenes to their barest, to flash character simply and starkly in front of us. We must not look for more than a second; we must hurry on. But to what?

Probably to some scene which has very little to do with character, with story, with any of the usual resting places, eminences, and consummations of the usual novel. The only thing that we are given to rest upon, to expand upon, to feel to the limits of our powers is some rapture of physical being. Such for instance is the scene when Paul and Miriam swing in the barn. Their bodies become incandescent, glowing, significant, as in other books a passage of emotion burns in that way. For the writer it seems the scene is possessed of a transcendental significance. Not in talk nor in story nor in death nor in love, but here as the body of the boy swings in the barn.

But, perhaps, because such a state cannot satisfy for long, perhaps because Lawrence lacks the final power which makes things entire in themselves, the effect of the book is that stability is never reached. The world of *Sons and Lovers* is perpetually in process of cohesion and dissolution. The magnet that tries to draw together the different particles of which the beautiful and vigorous world of Nottingham is made is this incandescent body, this beauty glowing in the flesh, this intense and burning light. Hence whatever we are shown seems to have a moment of its own. Nothing rests secure to be looked at. All is being sucked away by some dissatisfaction, some superior beauty, or desire, or possibility. The book therefore excites, irritates, moves, changes, seems full of stir and unrest and desire for something withheld, like the body of the hero. The whole world—it is a proof of the writer's remarkable strength—

is broken and tossed by the magnet of the young man who cannot bring the separate parts into a unity which will satisfy him.

This allows, partly at least, of a simple explanation. Paul Morel, like Lawrence himself, is the son of a miner. He is dissatisfied with his conditions. One of his first actions on selling a picture is to buy an evening suit. He is not a member, like Proust, of a settled and satisfied society. He is anxious to leave his own class and to enter another. He believes that the middle class possess what he does not possess. His natural honesty is too great to be satisfied with his mother's argument that the common people are better than the middle class because they possess more life. The middle class, Lawrence feels, possess ideas; or something else that he wishes himself to have. This is one cause of his unrest. And it is of profound importance. For the fact that he, like Paul, was a miner's son, and that he disliked his conditions, gave him a different approach to writing from those who have a settled station and enjoy circumstances which allow them to forget what those circumstances are.

Lawrence received a violent impetus from his birth. It set his gaze at an angle from which it took some of its most marked characteristics. He never looked back at the past, or at things as if they were curiosities of human psychology, nor was he interested in literature as literature. Everything has a use, a meaning, is not an end in itself. Comparing him again with Proust, one feels that he echoes nobody, continues no tradition, is unaware of the past, of the present save as it affects the future. As a writer, this lack of tradition affects him immensely. The thought plumps directly into his mind; up spurt the sentences as round, as hard, as direct as water thrown out in all directions by the impact of a stone. One feels that not a single word has been chosen for its beauty, or for its effect upon the architecture of the sentence.

Roger Fry

WHEN I was asked to open this exhibition of Roger Fry's
pictures my first instinct I admit was to refuse, for it
seemed to me that an exhibition of paintings ought to be
opened by a painter or by a critic of painting. But on second
thoughts it struck me that this particular exhibition, this
memorial exhibition of Roger Fry's pictures, might fitly be
opened by someone who is not a painter or a critic because
Roger Fry did more than anyone to make such people—such
outsiders—enjoy looking at pictures. That was my experience,
and I think I am right in saying that there are others in this
room who have felt the same thing. Pictures were to many of us
—if I may generalise—things that hung upon walls; silent
inscrutable patterns; treasure houses with locked doors in front
of which learned people would stop, and about which they
would lecture, saying that they were of this period or of that,
of this school or of that, probably by this master, but perhaps
on the other hand by one of his disciples. And we would trail
behind them, silent, servile, and bored. Then all of a sudden
those dim pictures began to flash with light and colour; and
our guides, those respectable professors, began to argue and to
quarrel, called each other—if I remember rightly—liars and
cheats, and altogether began to behave like living people
arguing about something of vital importance. What had happened? What had brought this life and colour, this racket and
din into the quiet galleries of ancient art? It was that Roger
Fry had gathered together the Post-Impressionist Exhibition
in Dover Street; and the names of Cézanne and Gauguin, of
Matisse and Picasso, suddenly became as hotly debated, as
violently defended as the names—shall we say?—of Ramsay
MacDonald, Hitler, or Lloyd George. That is many years ago.

An Address given at the opening of the Roger Fry Memorial
Exhibition at the Bristol Museum and Art Gallery on Friday, July
12th, 1935.

The dust of that conflict has died down. But all the same pictures have never gone back to their walls. They are no longer silent, decorous, and dull. They are things we live with, and laugh at, love and discuss. And I think I am right in saying that it was Roger Fry more than anybody who brought about this change. He did it, of course, by his writing and by his lecturing. Many of you will have read his books, and will have heard his lectures. You will know better than I can describe it how profoundly he felt about the roots of art; how subtly, with that long white wand of his, standing in front of his magic lantern, he would point to this line and to that and would bring to the surface in new and startling revelation those qualities that lie deep sunk in pictures so that we saw them afresh. You will have felt this while he lectured; you will still find it, happily, in his books; but I would like, if I can, to give you some faint idea how he did it in his talk.

I remember an instance that struck me greatly one night last summer. It was at a friend's house, and someone had brought him a picture for his opinion. It was a question whether it was a genuine picture by Degas, or whether it was an extremely skilful imitation. The picture was stood on a chair, and Roger Fry sat and looked at it. His eye ranged over it, carefully, appreciatively. It was a very good picture beyond a doubt; it was signed by Degas; it was in the manner of Degas—he was inclined to think on the whole that it was by Degas. And yet there was something that puzzled him; something—he could not say what—that made him hesitate. As if to rest himself, he turned away and took part in a discussion that was going forward in another corner of the room—a difficult discussion upon some abstract question of aesthetics. He argued and he listened to others arguing. But now and again I saw his eye go back to the picture as if it were feeling it, tasting it, making a voyage of discovery on its own. Then there was a pause. Suddenly he looked up and said: "No. No. That is not by Degas."

There it seemed to me one had a glimpse for a moment into the process that made him so great a critic. While he was arguing about the theory of art in the abstract his eye was ranging over the picture and bringing back its spoils. Then there was a moment of fusion, of comprehension; and his mind was made up. "No," he said. "It is not by Degas." But how was it done? By the union, it seemed to me, of two different qualities—his reason and his sensibility. Many people have one; many people have the other. But few have both, and fewer still are able to make them both work in harmony. But that was what he did. While he was reasoning he was seeing; and while he was seeing he was reasoning. He was acutely sensitive, but at the same time he was uncompromisingly honest. Was this integrity, this honesty, a quality that he owed in part to his Quaker blood? He came, as you know, of a great Quaker family, and I have sometimes thought that this clarity, this sobriety of judgment, this determination to get beneath the appearance to the bedrock beneath are qualities that go with a Quaker upbringing. At any rate he never allowed himself merely to feel; he always checked and verified his impressions. Whether he upset other people's views (as he did) or changed his own (and he did), he always used his brain to correct his sensibility. And what was of equal importance, he always allowed his sensibility to correct his brain.

Here I come to a point in speaking of him where I doubt if he would let me go on. For I want to say that his understanding of art owed much to his understanding of life, and yet I know that he disliked the mingling and mixing of different things. He wanted art to be art; literature to be literature; and life to be life. He was an undaunted enemy of the sloppiness, the vagueness, the sentimentality which has filled so many academies with anecdotes of dogs and duchesses. He detested the story-telling spirit which has clouded our painting and confused our criticism. But I will venture to say that one of the reasons why his criticism always grew, always went deeper, always included more, and never froze into the rigidity of death was that he himself breasted so many different currents of the stream of life. He was a man of many interests and many sympathies. As a young man he had been trained as a scientist. Science interested him profoundly. Poetry was one of his perpetual delights. He was deeply versed in French literature. He was a great lover of music. Anything that he could touch and handle and fashion with his fingers fascinated him. He made plates and pots with his own hands; he dyed stuffs; he designed furniture; he would come into the kitchen and teach the cook how to make an omelette; he would come into the drawing-room and teach the mistress how to arrange a bunch of flowers. And just as connoisseurs would bring him a picture for his opinion, so people of all kinds—and he had friends of all kinds —would bring him their lives—those canvases upon which we paint so many queer designs—and he would bring to bear upon their muddles and misfortunes the same rare mixture of logic and sympathy that made him so invigorating as a critic. He would start people living again just as he would start them painting again. And though I do not want to mix up different things, still I believe it was because so many interests, so many sympathies lived together in him that his teaching remained so fertile and so fresh.

But there was another reason why his criticism never became, as criticism so often does become, the repetition of a fixed idea. And that was of course that he always painted himself. He cared more for his painting than for his writing. The writing was done with many groans in the afternoon when the light was bad; on the tops of omnibuses; in the corners of third-class railway carriages. But painting was an instinct—a delight. If one were walking with him through the English fields, or driving with him along the roads of Italy or Greece, suddenly he would stop, and look. "I must just make a note of that," he would say, and out would come a pencil and a piece of paper and he would make a rough-and-ready sketch on the spot.

Many of the pictures on these walls are the results of those sketches. And because he painted himself he was perpetually forced to meet with his own brush those problems with which he was dealing with his pen. He knew from his own experience what labours, joys, despairs, go to the making of pictures. A picture was to him not merely the finished canvas but the canvas in the making. Every step of that struggle, which ends sometimes in victory, but more often in defeat, was known to him from his own daily battle. It was because he painted himself that he kept so keen a sense of all the intricate processes of painting; and that was why he had so high a standard of what I may call the morality of art. No one knew better than he did how hard it is to paint well; no one knew better than he did how easy it is to palm off upon the public something that does instead. That is why his criticism is so trenchant, so witty, often so devastating in its exposure of humbug and pretence. That too is why it is so full of respect and admiration for the artist who has used his gift honourably and honestly even though it is a small one.

He was never, I think, satisfied with his own painting; he never met with the success which he deserved. But that made no difference to his interest, to his activity. He went on painting; he went on tearing up his pictures; he threw them away; he began them again. And his devotion to his art seemed, if possible, to grow stronger with the years. Had he lived to be a hundred he would have been found, I am sure, sitting in front of a canvas with a brush in his hand.

Therefore there is nothing that he would have liked more than that you should have brought together this collection of his paintings. And there is no exhibition that could rouse questions of greater interest. We may ask ourselves, as we look at these pictures, is it a good thing that an artist should be also a critic, or does it inhibit his creative power? Is it necessary that an artist, in order to use his genius fully, should live half submerged in the dim world of ignorance, or on the contrary does knowledge and the consciousness that comes with it lead him to be more daring and more drastic in his researches and discoveries, and so prolong his artistic life and give it new power and direction? Such questions can be answered here as in no other room in England; for no artist, I think I am right in saying, knew more about the problems of his art than Roger Fry, or pursued them with a deeper curiosity or with greater courage.

But here I touch upon questions that lie beyond my scope—here I come to the pictures themselves; and I am not able to speak of Roger Fry's pictures as a fellow painter or as a fellow critic would speak of them. But speaking unprofessionally, as an outsider, I am sure that Roger Fry, were he here, would have made us all welcome equally to his exhibition. He would have asked only that we should come to it, whatever our calling, whatever our interests, with open eyes and open minds in the spirit of enjoyment. He believed that the love of art lives in most people if they will but give scope to it. He believed that the understanding of art, the enjoyment of art, are among the most profound and enduring pleasures that life has to give. I feel then that I am now asking you to embark upon a voyage—upon a voyage in which he will always be one of the great leaders, the great captains—a voyage of discovery into the mind and art of a remarkable man; and I have great pleasure in declaring this exhibition open.

The Art of Fiction

THAT fiction is a lady, and a lady who has somehow got herself into trouble, is a thought that must often have struck
her admirers. Many gallant gentlemen have ridden to her
rescue, chief among them Sir Walter Raleigh and Mr. Percy
Lubbock. But both were a little ceremonious in their approach;
both, one felt, had a great deal of knowledge of her, but not
much intimacy with her. Now comes Mr. Forster,[1] who dis-
claims knowledge but cannot deny that he knows the lady well.
If he lacks something of the others' authority, he enjoys the
privileges which are allowed the lover. He knocks at the bedroom door and is admitted when the lady is in slippers and
dressing-gown. Drawing up their chairs to the fire they talk
easily, wittily, subtly, like old friends who have no illusions,
although in fact the bedroom is a lecture-room and the place
the highly austere city of Cambridge.

This informal attitude on Mr. Forster's part is of course
deliberate. He is not a scholar; he refuses to be a pseudo-
scholar. There remains a point of view which the lecturer can
adopt usefully, if modestly. He can, as Mr. Forster puts it,
"visualise the English novelists not as floating down that stream
which bears all its sons away unless they are careful, but as
seated together in a room, a circular room—a sort of British
Museum reading - room — all writing their novels simultaneously". So simultaneous are they, indeed, that they persist in writing out of their turn. Richardson insists that he is
contemporary with Henry James. Wells will write a passage
which might be written by Dickens. Being a novelist himself,
Mr. Forster is not annoyed at this discovery. He knows from
experience what a muddled and illogical machine the brain of
a writer is. He knows how little they think about methods; how
completely they forget their grandfathers; how absorbed they

Written in 1927
[1] *Aspects of the Novel*, by E. M. Forster.

tend to become in some vision of their own. Thus, though the scholars have all his respect, his sympathies are with the untidy and harassed people who are scribbling away at their books. And looking down on them, not from any great height, but, as he says, over their shoulders, he makes out, as he passes, that certain shapes and ideas tend to recur in their minds whatever their period. Since story-telling began stories have always been made of much the same elements; and these, which he calls The Story, People, Plot, Fantasy, Prophecy, Pattern, and Rhythm, he now proceeds to examine.

Many are the judgments that we would willingly argue, many are the points over which we would willingly linger, as Mr. Forster passes lightly on his way. That Scott is a story-teller and nothing more; that a story is the lowest of literary organisms; that the novelist's unnatural preoccupation with love is largely a reflection of his own state of mind while he composes—every page has a hint or a suggestion which makes us stop to think or wish to contradict. Never raising his voice above the speaking level, Mr. Forster has the art of saying things which sink airily enough into the mind to stay there and unfurl like those Japanese flowers which open up in the depths of the water. But greatly though these sayings intrigue us, we want to call a halt at some definite stopping place; we want to make Mr. Forster stand and deliver. For possibly, if fiction is, as we suggest, in difficulties, it may be because nobody grasps her firmly and defines her severely. She has had no rules drawn up for her, very little thinking done on her behalf. And though rules may be wrong and must be broken, they have this advantage—they confer dignity and order upon their subject; they admit her to a place in civilised society; they prove that she is worthy of consideration. But this part of his duty, if it is his duty, Mr. Forster expressly disowns. He is not going to theorise about fiction except incidentally; he doubts even whether she is to be approached by a critic, and if so, with what critical equipment. All we can do is to edge him into a position which is definite enough for us to see where he stands. And perhaps the best way to do this is to quote, much summarised, his estimates of three great figures—Meredith, Hardy, and Henry James. Meredith is an exploded philosopher. His vision of nature is "fluffy and lush". When he gets serious and noble he becomes a bully. "And his novels; most of the social values are faked. The tailors are not tailors, the cricket matches are not cricket." Hardy is a far greater writer. But he is not so successful as a novelist because his characters are "required to contribute too much to the plot; except in their rustic humours their vitality has been impoverished, they have gone thin and dry—he has emphasised causality more strongly than his medium permits". Henry James pursued the narrow path of aesthetic duty and was successful. But at what a sacrifice? "Most of human life has to disappear before he can do us a novel. Maimed creatures can alone breathe in his novels. His characters are few in number and constructed on stingy lines."

Now if we look at these judgments, and place beside them certain admissions and omissions, we shall see that if we cannot pin Mr. Forster to a creed we can commit him to a point of view. There is something—we hesitate to be more precise—which he calls "life". It is to this that he brings the books of Meredith, Hardy, or James for comparison. Always their failure is some failure in relation to life. It is the humane as opposed to the aesthetic view of fiction. It maintains that the novel is "sogged with humanity"; that "human beings have their great chance in the novel"; a triumph won at the expense of life is in fact a defeat. Thus we arrive at the notably harsh judgment of Henry James. For Henry James brought into the novel something besides human beings. He created patterns which, though beautiful in themselves, are hostile to humanity. And for his neglect of life, says Mr. Forster, he will perish.

But at this point the pertinacious pupil may demand: "What is this 'Life' that keeps on cropping up so mysteriously and so complacently in books about fiction? Why is it absent in a pattern and present in a tea party? Why is the pleasure that we get from the pattern in *The Golden Bowl* less valuable than the emotion which Trollope gives us when he describes a lady drinking tea in a parsonage? Surely the definition of life is too arbitrary, and requires to be expanded." To all of this Mr. Forster would reply, presumably, that he lays down no laws; the novel somehow seems to him too soft a substance to be carved like the other arts; he is merely telling us what moves him and what leaves him cold. Indeed, there is no other criterion. So then we are back in the old bog; nobody knows anything about the laws of fiction; or what its relation is to life; or to what effects it can lend itself. We can only trust our instincts. If instinct leads one reader to call Scott a story-teller, another to call him a master of romance; if one reader is moved by art, another by life, each is right, and each can pile a card-house of theory on top of his opinion as high as he can go. But the assumption that fiction is more intimately and humbly attached to the service of human beings than the other arts leads to a further position which Mr. Forster's book again illustrates. It is unnecessary to dwell upon her aesthetic functions because they are so feeble that they can safely be ignored. Thus, though it is impossible to imagine a book on painting in which not a word should be said about the medium in which a painter works, a wise and brilliant book, like Mr. Forster's, can be written about fiction without saying more than a sentence or two about the medium in which a novelist works. Almost nothing is said about words. One might suppose, unless one had read them, that a sentence means the same thing and is used for the same purposes by Sterne and by Wells. One might conclude that *Tristram Shandy* gains nothing from the language in which it is written. So with the other aesthetic qualities. Pattern, as we have seen, is recognised, but savagely censured for her tendency to obscure the human features. Beauty occurs but she is suspect. She makes one furtive appearance—"beauty at which a novelist should never aim, though he fails if he does not achieve it"—and the possibility that she may emerge again as rhythm is briefly discussed in a few interesting pages at the end. But for the rest fiction is treated as a parasite which draws sustenance from life and must in gratitude resemble life or perish. In poetry, in drama, words may excite and stimulate and deepen without this allegiance; but in fiction they must first and foremost hold themselves at the service of the teapot and the pug dog, and to be found wanting is to be found lacking.

Strange though this unaesthetic attitude would be in the critic of any other art, it does not surprise us in the critic of fiction. For one thing, the problem is extremely difficult. A book fades like a mist, like a dream. How are we to take a stick and point to that tone, that relation, in the vanishing pages, as Mr. Roger Fry points with his wand at a line or a colour in the picture displayed before him? Moreover, a novel in particular has roused a thousand ordinary human feelings in its progress. To drag in art in such a connection seems priggish and cold-hearted. It may well compromise the critic as a man of feeling and domestic ties. And so while the painter, the musician, and the poet come in for their share of criticism, the novelist goes unscathed. His character will be discussed; his morality, it may be his genealogy, will be examined; but his writing will go scot-free. There is not a critic alive now who will say that a novel is a work of art and that as such he will judge it.

And perhaps, as Mr. Forster insinuates, the critics are right. In England at any rate the novel is not a work of art. There are none to be stood beside *War and Peace*, *The Brothers Karamazov*, or *A la Recherche du Temps Perdu*. But while we accept the fact, we cannot suppress one last conjecture. In France and Russia they take fiction seriously. Flaubert spends a month seeking a phrase to describe a cabbage. Tolstoy writes *War and Peace* seven times over. Something of their pre-eminence may be due to the pains they take, something to the severity with which they are judged. If the English critic were less domestic, less assiduous to protect the rights of what it pleases him to call life, the novelist might be bolder too. He might cut adrift from the eternal tea-table and the plausible and preposterous formulas which are supposed to represent the whole of our human adventure. But then the story might wobble; the plot might crumble; ruin might seize upon the characters. The novel, in short, might become a work of art.

Such are the dreams that Mr. Forster leads us to cherish. For his is a book to encourage dreaming. None more suggestive has been written about the poor lady whom, with perhaps mistaken chivalry, we still persist in calling the art of fiction.

American Fiction

E XCURSIONS into the literature of a foreign country much resemble our travels abroad. Sights that are taken for granted by the inhabitants seem to us astonishing; however well we seemed to know the language at home, it sounds differently on the lips of those who have spoken it from birth; and above all, in our desire to get at the heart of the country we seek out whatever it may be that is most unlike what we are used to, and declaring this to be the very essence of the French or American genius proceed to lavish upon it a credulous devotion, to build up upon it a structure of theory which may well amuse, annoy, or even momentarily enlighten those who are French or American by birth.

The English tourist in American literature wants above all things something different from what he has at home. For this reason the one American writer whom the English wholeheartedly admire is Walt Whitman. There, you will hear them say, is the real American undisguised. In the whole of English literature there is no figure which resembles his—among all our poetry none in the least comparable to *Leaves of Grass*. This very unlikeness becomes a merit, and leads us, as we steep ourselves in the refreshing unfamiliarity, to become less and less able to appreciate Emerson, Lowell, Hawthorne, who have had their counterparts among us and drew their culture from our books. The obsession, whether well or ill founded, fair or unfair in its results, persists at the present moment. To dismiss such distinguished names as those of Henry James, Mr. Hergesheimer, and Mrs. Wharton would be impossible; but their praises are qualified with the reservation—they are not Americans; they do not give us anything that we have not got already.

Thus having qualified the tourist's attitude, in its crudity and onesidedness, let us begin our excursion into modern

Written in 1925

94

American fiction by asking what are the sights we ought to see. Here our bewilderment begins; for the names of so many authors, the titles of so many books, rise at once to the lips. Mr. Dreiser, Mr. Cabell, Miss Canfield, Mr. Sherwood Anderson, Miss Hurst, Mr. Sinclair Lewis, Miss Willa Cather, Mr. Ring Lardner—all have done work which, if time allowed, we should do well to examine carefully, and, if we must concentrate upon two or three at most, it is because, travellers and tourists as we are, it seems best to sketch a theory of the tendency of American fiction from the inspection of a few important books rather than to examine each writer separately by himself. Of all American novelists the most discussed and read in England at the present moment are probably Mr. Sherwood Anderson and Mr. Sinclair Lewis. And among all their fiction we find one volume, *A Story Teller's Story*, which, being fact rather than fiction, may serve as interpreter, may help us to guess the nature of American writers' problems before we see them tussled with or solved. Peering over Mr. Sherwood Anderson's shoulder, we may get a preliminary view of the world as it looks to the novelist before it is disguised and arranged for the reception of his characters. Indeed, if we look over Mr. Anderson's shoulder, America appears a very strange place. What is it that we see here? A vast continent, scattered here and there with brand new villages which nature has not absorbed into herself with ivy and moss, summer and winter, as in England, but man has built recently, hastily, economically, so that the village is like the suburb of a town. The slow English wagons are turned into Ford cars; the primrose banks have become heaps of old tins; the barns sheds of corrugated iron. It is cheap, it is new, it is ugly, it is made of odds and ends, hurriedly flung together, loosely tied in temporary cohesion—that is the burden of Mr. Anderson's complaint. And, he proceeds to ask, how can the imagination of an artist take root here, where the soil is stony and the imagination stubs itself upon the rocks? There is one solution and one only —by being resolutely and defiantly American. Explicitly and implicitly that is the conclusion he reaches; that is the note which turns the discord to harmony. Mr. Anderson is for ever repeating over and over like a patient hypnotising himself, "I am the American man". The words rise in his mind with the persistency of a submerged but fundamental desire. Yes, he is the American man; it is a terrible misfortune; it is an enormous opportunity; but for good or for bad, he is the American man. "Behold in me the American man striving to become an artist, to become conscious of himself, filled with wonder concerning himself and others, trying to have a good time and not fake a good time. I am not English, Italian, Jew, German, Frenchman, Russian. What am I?" Yes, we may be excused for repeating, what is he? One thing is certain—whatever the American man may be, he is not English; whatever he may become, he will not become an Englishman.

For that is the first step in the process of being American—to be not English. The first step in the education of an American writer is to dismiss the whole army of English words which have marched so long under the command of dead English generals. He must tame and compel to his service the "little American words"; he must forget all that he learnt in the school of Fielding and Thackeray; he must learn to write as he talks to men in Chicago bar-rooms, to men in the factories of Indiana. That is the first step; but the next step is far more difficult. For having decided what he is not, he must proceed to discover what he is. This is the beginning of a stage of acute self-consciousness which manifests itself in writers otherwise poles asunder. Nothing, indeed, surprises the English tourist more than the prevalence of this self-consciousness and the bitterness, for the most part against England, with which it is accompanied. One is reminded constantly of the attitude of another race, till lately subject and still galled by the memory of its chains. Women writers have to meet many of the same problems that beset Americans. They too are conscious of their own peculiarities as a sex; apt to suspect insolence, quick to avenge grievances, eager to shape an art of their own. In both cases all kinds of consciousness—consciousness of self, of race, of sex, of civilisation—which have nothing to do with art, have got between them and the paper, with results that are, on the surface at least, unfortunate. It is easy enough to see that Mr. Anderson, for example, would be a much more perfect artist if he could forget that he is an American; he would write better prose if he could use all words impartially, new or old, English or American, classical or slang.

Nevertheless as we turn from his autobiography to his fiction we are forced to own (as some women writers also make us own) that to come fresh to the world, to turn a new angle to the light, is so great an achievement that for its sake we can pardon the bitterness, the self-consciousness, the angularity which inevitably go with it. In *The Triumph of the Egg* there is some rearrangement of the old elements of art which makes us rub our eyes. The feeling recalls that with which we read Chekhov for the first time. There are no familiar handles to lay hold of in *The Triumph of the Egg*. The stories baffle our efforts, slip through our fingers and leave us feeling, not that it is Mr. Anderson who has failed us, but that we as readers have muffed our work and must go back, like chastened schoolchildren, and spell the lesson over again in the attempt to lay hold of the meaning.

Mr. Anderson has bored into that deeper and warmer layer of human nature which it would be frivolous to ticket new or old, American or European. In his determination to be "true to the essence of things" he has fumbled his way into something genuine, persistent, of universal significance, in proof of which he has done what, after all, very few writers succeed in doing— he has made a world of his own. It is a world in which the senses flourish; it is dominated by instincts rather than by ideas; racehorses make the hearts of little boys beat high; cornfields flow around the cheap towns like golden seas, illimitable and profound; everywhere boys and girls are dreaming of voyages and adventures, and this world of sensuality and instinctive desire is clothed in a warm cloudy atmosphere, wrapped about in a soft caressing envelope, which always seems a little too loose to fit the shape. Pointing to the formlessness of Mr. Anderson's work, the vagueness of his language, his tendency to land his stories softly in a bog, the English tourist would say that all this confirms him in his theory of what is to be expected of an American writer of insight and sincerity. The softness, the shellessness of Mr. Anderson are inevitable since he has scooped out from the heart of America matter which has never been confined in a shell before. He is too much enamoured of this precious stuff to squeeze it into any of those old and intricate poems which the art and industry of Europe have secreted. Rather he will leave what he has found exposed, defenceless, naked to scorn and laughter.

But if this theory holds good of the work of American novelists, how then are we to account for the novels of Mr. Sinclair Lewis? Does it not explode at the first touch of *Babbitt* and *Main Street* and *Our Mr. Wrenn* like a soap bubble dashed against the edge of a hard mahogany wardrobe? For it is precisely by its hardness, its efficiency, its compactness that Mr. Lewis's work excels. Yet he also is an American; he also has devoted book after book to the description and elucidation of America. Far from being shelless, however, his books, one is inclined to say, are all shell; the only doubt is whether he has left any room for the snail. At any rate *Babbitt* completely refutes the theory that an American writer, writing about America, must necessarily lack the finish, the technique, the power to model and control his material which one might suppose to be the bequest of an old civilisation to its artists. In all these respects, *Babbitt* is the equal of any novel written in English in the present century. The tourist therefore must make his choice between two alternatives. Either there is no profound difference between English and American writers, and their experience is so similar that it can be housed in the same form; or Mr. Lewis has modelled himself so closely upon the English—H. G. Wells is a very obvious master—that he has sacrificed his American characteristics in the process. But the art of reading would be simpler and less adventurous than it is if writers could be parcelled out in strips of green and blue. Study of Mr. Lewis more and more convinces us that the surface appearance of downright decision is deceptive; the outer composure hardly holds together the warring elements within; the colours have run.

For though *Babbitt* would appear as solid and authentic a portrait of the American business man as can well be painted, certain doubts run across us and shake our conviction. But, we may ask, where all is so masterly, self-assured, and confident, what foothold can there be for doubt to lodge upon? To begin with we doubt Mr. Lewis himself: we doubt, that is to say, that he is nearly as sure of himself or of his subject as he would have us believe. For he, too, though in a way very different from Mr. Anderson's way, is writing with one eye on Europe, a division of attention which the reader is quick to feel and resent. He too has the American self-consciousness, though it is masterfully suppressed and allowed only to utter itself once or twice in a sharp cry of bitterness ("Babbitt was as much amused by the antiquated provincialism as any proper Englishman by any American"). But the uneasiness is there. He has not identified himself with America; rather he has constituted himself the guide and interpreter between the Americans and the English, and, as he conducts his party of Europeans over the typical American city (of which he is a native) and shows them the typical American citizen (to whom he is related) he is equally divided between shame at what he has to show and anger at the Europeans for laughing at it. Zenith is a despicable place, but the English are even more despicable for despising it.

In such an atmosphere intimacy is impossible. All that a writer of Mr. Lewis's powers can do is to be unflinchingly accurate and more and more on his guard against giving himself away. Accordingly, never was so complete a model of a city made before. We turn on the taps and the water runs; we press a button and cigars are lit and beds warmed. But this glorification of machinery, this lust for "toothpastes, socks, tires, cameras, instantaneous hot water bottles . . . at first the signs, then the substitutes for joy and passion and wisdom" is only a device for putting off the evil day which Mr. Lewis sees looming ahead. However he may dread what people will think of him, he must give himself away. Babbitt must be proved to possess some share in truth and beauty, some character, some emotion of his own, or Babbitt will be nothing but an improved device for running motor cars, a convenient surface for the display of mechanical ingenuity. To make us care for Babbitt—that was his problem. With this end in view Mr. Lewis shamefacedly assures us that Babbitt has his dreams. Stout though he is, this elderly business man dreams of a fairy child waiting at a gate. "Her dear and tranquil hand caressed his cheek. He was gallant and wise and well-beloved; warm ivory were her arms; and beyond perilous moors the brave sea glittered." But that is not a dream; that is simply the protest of a man who has never dreamed in his life, but is determined to prove that dreaming is as easy as shelling peas. What are dreams made of—the most expensive dreams? Seas, fairies, moors? Well, he will have a little of each, and if that is not a dream, he seems to demand, jumping out of bed in a fury, what then is it? With sex relations and family affection he is much more at ease. Indeed it would be impossible to deny that if we put our ears to his shell, the foremost citizen in Zenith can be heard moving cumbrously but unmistakably within. One has moments of affection for him, moments of sympathy and even of desire that some miracle may happen, the rock be cleft asunder, and the living creature, with his capacity for fun, suffering, and happiness, be set at liberty. But no; his movements are too sluggish; Babbitt will never escape; he will die in his prison, bequeathing only the chance of escape to his son.

In some such way as this, then, the English tourist makes his theory embrace both Mr. Anderson and Mr. Sinclair Lewis. Both suffer as novelists from being American; Mr. Anderson, because he must protest his pride; Mr. Lewis, because he must conceal his bitterness. Mr. Anderson's way is the less injurious to him as an artist, and his imagination is the more vigorous of the two. He has gained more than he has lost by being the spokesman of a new country, the worker in fresh clay. Mr. Lewis it would seem was meant by nature to take his place with Mr. Wells and Mr. Bennett, and had he been born in England would undoubtedly have proved himself the equal of these two famous men. Denied, however, the richness of an old civilisation —the swarm of ideas upon which the art of Mr. Wells has battened, the solidity of custom which has nourished the art of Mr. Bennett—he has been forced to criticise rather than to explore, and the object of his criticism—the civilisation of Zenith—was unfortunately too meagre to sustain him. Yet a little reflection, and a comparison between Mr. Anderson and Mr. Lewis, put a different colour on our conclusion. Look at Americans as an American, see Mrs. Opal Emerson Mudge as she is herself, not as a type and symbol of America displayed for the amusement of the condescending Britisher, and then, we dimly suspect, Mrs. Mudge is no type, no scarecrow, no abstraction. Mrs. Mudge is—but it is not for an English writer to say what. He can only peep and peer between the chinks of the barrier and hazard the opinion that Mrs. Mudge and the Americans generally are, somehow, human beings into the bargain.

That suspicion suddenly becomes a certainty as we read the first pages of Mr. Ring Lardner's *You Know Me, Al*, and the change is bewildering. Hitherto we have been kept at arm's length, reminded constantly of our superiority, of our inferiority, of the fact, anyhow, that we are alien blood and bone. But Mr. Lardner is not merely unaware that we differ; he is unaware that we exist. When a crack player is in the middle of an exciting game of baseball he does not stop to wonder whether the audience likes the colour of his hair. All his mind is on the game. So Mr. Lardner does not waste a moment when he writes in thinking whether he is using American slang or Shakespeare's English; whether he is remembering Fielding or forgetting Fielding; whether he is proud of being American or ashamed of not being Japanese; all his mind is on the story. Hence all our minds are on the story. Hence, incidentally, he writes the best prose that has come our way. Hence we feel at last freely admitted to the society of our fellows.

That this should be true of *You Know Me, Al*, a story about baseball, a game which is not played in England, a story written often in a language which is not English, gives us pause. To what does he owe his success? Besides his unconsciousness and the additional power which he is thus free to devote to his art, Mr. Lardner has talents of a remarkable order. With extraordinary ease and aptitude, with the quickest strokes, the surest touch, the sharpest insight, he lets Jack Keefe the baseball player cut out his own outline, fill in his own depths, until the figure of the foolish, boastful, innocent athlete lives before us. As he babbles out his mind on paper there rise up friends, sweethearts, the scenery, town, and country—all surround him and make him up in his completeness. We gaze into the depths of a society which goes its ways intent on its own concerns. There, perhaps, is one of the elements of Mr. Lardner's success. He is not merely himself intent on his own game, but his characters are equally intent on theirs. It is no coincidence that the best of Mr. Lardner's stories are about games, for one may guess that Mr. Lardner's interest in games has solved one of the most difficult problems of the American writer; it has given him a clue, a centre, a meeting place for the divers activities of people whom a vast continent isolates, whom no tradition controls. Games give him what society gives his English brother. Whatever the precise reason, Mr. Lardner at any rate provides something unique in its kind, something indigenous to the soil, which the traveller may carry off as a trophy to prove to the incredulous that he has actually been to America and found it a foreign land. But the time has come when the tourist must reckon up his expenses and experiences, and attempt to cast up his account of the tour as a whole.

At the outset let us admit that our impressions are highly mixed and the opinions we have come to, if anything, less definite, less assured than those with which we started. For when we consider the mixed origin of the literature we are trying to understand, its youth, its age, and all those currents which are blowing across the stream of its natural development, we may well exclaim that French is simpler, English is simpler, all modern literatures are simpler to sum up and understand than this new American literature. A discord lies at the root of it; the natural bent of the American is twisted at the start. For the more sensitive he is, the more he must read English literature; the more he reads English literature, the more alive he must become to the puzzle and perplexity of this great art which uses the language on his own lips to express an experience which is not his and to mirror a civilisation which he has never known. The choice has to be made—whether to yield or to rebel. The more sensitive, or at least the more sophisticated, the Henry Jameses, the Hergesheimers, the Edith Whartons, decide in favour of England and pay the penalty by exaggerating the English culture, the traditional English good manners, and stressing too heavily or in the wrong places those social differences which, though the first to strike the foreigner, are by no means the most profound. What their work gains in refinement it loses in that perpetual distortion of values, that obsession with surface distinctions—the age of old houses, the glamour of great names—which makes it necessary to remember that Henry James was a foreigner if we are not to call him a snob.

On the other hand, the simpler and cruder writers, like Walt Whitman, Mr. Anderson, Mr. Masters—decide in favour of America, but truculently, self-consciously, protestingly, "showing off" as the nurses would say, their newness, their independence, their individuality. Both influences are unfortunate and serve to obscure and delay the development of the real American literature itself. But, some critics would interpose, are we not making mountains out of molehills, conjuring up distinctions where none exist? The "real American literature" in the time of Hawthorne, Emerson, and Lowell was much of a piece with contemporary English literature, and the present movement towards a national literature is confined to a few enthusiasts and extremists who will grow older and wiser and see the folly of their ways.

But the tourist can no longer accept this comfortable doctrine, flattering though it be to his pride of birth. Obviously there are American writers who do not care a straw for English opinion or for English culture, and write very vigorously none the less—witness Mr. Lardner; there are Americans who have all the accomplishments of culture without a trace of its excess —witness Miss Willa Cather; there are Americans whose aim it is to write a book off their own bat and no one else's—witness Miss Fannie Hurst. But the shortest tour, the most superficial inspection, must impress him with what is of far greater importance—the fact that where the land itself is so different, and the society so different, the literature must needs differ, and differ more and more widely as time goes by, from those of other countries.

American literature will be influenced, no doubt, like all others, and the English influence may well predominate. But clearly the English tradition is already unable to cope with this vast land, these prairies, these cornfields, these lonely little groups of men and women scattered at immense distances from each other, these vast industrial cities with their skyscrapers and their night signs and their perfect organisation of machinery. It cannot extract their meaning and interpret their beauty. How could it be otherwise? The English tradition is formed upon a little country; its centre is an old house with many rooms each crammed with objects and crowded with people who know each other intimately, whose manners, thoughts, and speech are ruled all the time, if unconsciously, by the spirit of the past. But in America there is baseball instead of society; instead of the old landscape which has moved men to emotion for endless summers and springs, a new land, its tin cans, its prairies, its cornfields flung disorderly about like a mosaic of incongruous pieces waiting order at the artist's hands; while the people are equally diversified into fragments of many nationalities.

To describe, to unify, to make order out of all these severed parts, a new art is needed and the control of a new tradition. That both are in process of birth the language itself gives us proof. For the Americans are doing what the Elizabethans did—they are coining new words. They are instinctively making the language adapt itself to their needs. In England, save for the impetus given by the war, the word-coining power has lapsed; our writers vary the metres of their poetry, remodel the rhythms of prose, but one may search English fiction in vain for a single new word. It is significant that when we want to freshen our speech we borrow from America—poppycock, rambunctious, flipflop, booster, good-mixer—all the expressive ugly vigorous slang which creeps into use among us first in talk, later in writing, comes from across the Atlantic. Nor does it need much foresight to predict that when words are being made, a literature will be made out of them. Already we hear the first jars and dissonances, the strangled difficult music of the prelude. As we shut our books and look out again upon the English fields a strident note rings in our ears. We hear the first lovemaking and the first laughter of the child who was exposed by its parents three hundred years ago upon a rocky shore and survived solely by its own exertions and is a little sore and proud and diffident and self-assertive in consequence and is now on the threshold of man's estate.

The Leaning Tower

A WRITER is a person who sits at a desk and keeps his eye fixed, as intently as he can, upon a certain object—that figure of speech may help to keep us steady on our path if we look at it for a moment. He is an artist who sits with a sheet of paper in front of him trying to copy what he sees. What is his object—his model? Nothing so simple as a painter's model; it is not a bowl of flowers, a naked figure, or a dish of apples and onions. Even the simplest story deals with more than one person, with more than one time. Characters begin young; they grow old; they move from scene to scene, from place to place. A writer has to keep his eye upon a model that moves, that changes, upon an object that is not one object but innumerable objects. Two words alone cover all that a writer looks at—they are, human life.

Let us look at the writer next. What do we see—only a person who sits with a pen in his hand in front of a sheet of paper? That tells us little or nothing. And we know very little. Considering how much we talk about writers, how much they talk about themselves, it is odd how little we know about them. Why are they so common sometimes; then so rare? Why do they sometimes write nothing but masterpieces, then nothing but trash? And why should a family, like the Shelleys, like the Keatses, like the Brontës, suddenly burst into flame and bring to birth Shelley, Keats, and the Brontës? What are the conditions that bring about that explosion? There is no answer —naturally. Since we have not yet discovered the germ of influenza, how should we yet have discovered the germ of genius? We know even less about the mind than about the body. We have less evidence. It is less than two hundred years since people took an interest in themselves; Boswell was almost the first writer who thought that a man's life was worth writing

A paper read to the Workers' Educational Association, Brighton, May 1940.

a book about. Until we have more facts, more biographies, more autobiographies, we cannot know much about ordinary people, let alone about extraordinary people. Thus at present we have only theories about writers—a great many theories, but they all differ. The politician says that a writer is the product of the society in which he lives, as a screw is the product of a screw machine; the artist, that a writer is a heavenly apparition that slides across the sky, grazes the earth, and vanishes. To the psychologists a writer is an oyster; feed him on gritty facts, irritate him with ugliness, and by way of compensation, as they call it, he will produce a pearl. The genealogists say that certain stocks, certain families, breed writers as fig trees breed figs—Dryden, Swift, and Pope they tell us were all cousins. This proves that we are in the dark about writers; anybody can make a theory; the germ of a theory is almost always the wish to prove what the theorist wishes to believe.

Theories then are dangerous things. All the same we must risk making one this afternoon since we are going to discuss modern tendencies. Directly we speak of tendencies or movements we commit ourselves to the belief that there is some force, influence, outer pressure which is strong enough to stamp itself upon a whole group of different writers so that all their writing has a certain common likeness. We must then have a theory as to what this influence is. But let us always remember—influences are infinitely numerous; writers are infinitely sensitive; each writer has a different sensibility. That is why literature is always changing, like the weather, like the clouds in the sky. Read a page of Scott; then of Henry James; try to work out the influences that have transformed the one page into the other. It is beyond our skill. We can only hope therefore to single out the most obvious influences that have formed writers into groups. Yet there are groups. Books descend from books as families descend from families. Some descend from Jane Austen; others from Dickens. They resemble their parents, as human children resemble their parents; yet they differ as children differ, and revolt as children revolt. Perhaps it will be easier to understand living writers as we take a quick look at some of their forebears. We have not time to go far back—certainly we have not time to look closely. But let us glance at English

writers as they were a hundred years ago—that may help us to
see what we ourselves look like.

In 1815 England was at war, as England is now. And it is
natural to ask, how did their war—the Napoleonic war—affect
them? Was that one of the influences that formed them into
groups? The answer is a very strange one. The Napoleonic wars
did not affect the great majority of those writers at all. The
proof of that is to be found in the work of two great novelists—
Jane Austen and Walter Scott. Each lived through the
Napoleonic wars; each wrote through them. But, though
novelists live very close to the life of their time, neither of them
in all their novels mentioned the Napoleonic wars. This shows
that their model, their vision of human life, was not disturbed
or agitated or changed by war. Nor were they themselves. It is
easy to see why that was so. Wars were then remote; wars were
carried on by soldiers and sailors, not by private people. The
rumour of battles took a long time to reach England. It was
only when the mail coaches clattered along the country roads
hung with laurels that the people in villages like Brighton knew
that a victory had been won and lit their candles and stuck
them in their windows. Compare that with our state to-day.
To-day we hear the gunfire in the Channel. We turn on the
wireless; we hear an airman telling us how this very afternoon
he shot down a raider; his machine caught fire; he plunged into
the sea; the light turned green and then black; he rose to the
top and was rescued by a trawler. Scott never saw the sailors
drowning at Trafalgar; Jane Austen never heard the cannon
roar at Waterloo. Neither of them heard Napoleon's voice as
we hear Hitler's voice as we sit at home of an evening.

That immunity from war lasted all through the nineteenth
century. England, of course, was often at war—there was the
Crimean War; the Indian Mutiny; all the little Indian frontier
wars, and at the end of the century the Boer War. Keats,
Shelley, Byron, Dickens, Thackeray, Carlyle, Ruskin, the
Brontës, George Eliot, Trollope, the Brownings—all lived
through all those wars. But did they ever mention them? Only
Thackeray, I think; in *Vanity Fair* he described the Battle of
Waterloo long after it was fought; but only as an illustration,
as a scene. It did not change his characters' lives; it merely

killed one of his heroes. Of the poets, only Byron and Shelley felt the influence of the nineteenth-century wars profoundly. War then we can say, speaking roughly, did not affect either the writer or his vision of human life in the nineteenth century. But peace—let us consider the influence of peace. Were the nineteenth-century writers affected by the settled, the peaceful and prosperous state of England? Let us collect a few facts before we launch out into the dangers and delights of theory. We know for a fact, from their lives, that the nineteenth-century writers were all of them fairly well-to-do middle-class people. Most had been educated either at Oxford or at Cambridge. Some were civil servants like Trollope and Matthew Arnold. Others, like Ruskin, were professors. It is a fact that their work brought them considerable fortunes. There is visible proof of that in the houses they built. Look at Abbotsford, bought out of the proceeds of Scott's novels; or at Farringford, built by Tennyson from his poetry. Look at Dickens's great house in Marylebone; and at his great house at Gadshill. All these are houses needing many butlers, maids, gardeners, grooms to keep the tables spread, the cans carried, and the gardens neat and fruitful. Not only did they leave behind them large houses; they left too an immense body of literature— poems, plays, novels, essays, histories, criticism. It was a very prolific, creative, rich century—the nineteenth century. Now let us ask—is there any connection between that material prosperity and that intellectual creativeness? Did one lead to the other? How difficult it is to say—for we know so little about writers, and what conditions help them, what hinder them. It is only a guess, and a rough guess; yet I think that there is a connection. "I think"—perhaps it would be nearer the truth to say "I see". Thinking should be based on facts; and here we have intuitions rather than facts—the lights and shades that come after books are read, the general shifting surface of a large expanse of print. What I see, glancing over that shifting surface, is the picture I have already shown you; the writer seated in front of human life in the nineteenth century; and, looking at it through their eyes, I see that life divided up, herded together, into many different classes. There is the aristocracy; the landed gentry; the professional class; the commercial class; the working class; and there, in one dark blot, is that great class which is called simply and comprehensively "The Poor". To the nineteenth-century writer human life must have looked like a landscape cut up into separate fields. In each field was gathered a different group of people. Each to some extent had its own traditions; its own manners; its own speech; its own dress; its own occupation. But owing to that peace, to that prosperity, each group was tethered, stationary—a herd grazing within its own hedges. And the nineteenth-century writer did not seek to change those divisions; he accepted them. He accepted them so completely that he became unconscious of them. Does that serve to explain why it is that the nineteenth-century writers are able to create so many characters who are not types but individuals? Is it because he did not see the hedges that divide classes; he saw only the human beings that live within those hedges? Is that why he could get beneath the surface and create many-sided characters—Pecksniff, Becky Sharp, Mr. Woodhouse—who change with the years, as the living change? To us now the hedges are visible. We can see now that each of those writers only dealt with a very small section of human life—all Thackeray's characters are upper middle-class people; all Dickens's characters come from the lower or middle class. We can see that now; but the writer himself seems unconscious that he is only dealing with one type; with the type formed by the class into which the writer was born himself, with which he is most familiar. And that unconsciousness was an immense advantage to him.

Unconsciousness, which means presumably that the under-mind works at top speed while the upper-mind drowses, is a state we all know. We all have experience of the work done by unconsciousness in our own daily lives. You have had a crowded day, let us suppose, sightseeing in London. Could you say what you had seen and done when you came back? Was it not all a blur, a confusion? But after what seemed a rest, a chance to turn aside and look at something different, the sights and sounds and sayings that had been of most interest to you swam to the surface, apparently of their own accord; and remained in memory; what was unimportant sank into forget-fulness. So it is with the writer. After a hard day's work,

trudging round, seeing all he can, feeling all he can, taking in
the book of his mind innumerable notes, the writer becomes—
if he can—unconscious. In fact, his under-mind works at top
speed while his upper-mind drowses. Then, after a pause the
veil lifts; and there is the thing—the thing he wants to write
about—simplified, composed. Do we strain Wordsworth's
famous saying about emotion recollected in tranquillity when
we infer that by tranquillity he meant that the writer needs to
become unconscious before he can create?

If we want to risk a theory, then, we can say that peace and
prosperity were influences that gave the nineteenth-century
writers a family likeness. They had leisure; they had security;
life was not going to change; they themselves were not going to
change. They could look; and look away. They could forget;
and then—in their books—remember. Those then are some of
the conditions that brought about a certain family likeness, in
spite of the great individual differences, among the nineteenth-
century writers. The nineteenth century ended; but the same
conditions went on. They lasted, roughly speaking, till the year
1914. Even in 1914 we can still see the writer sitting as he sat
all through the nineteenth century looking at human life; and
that human life is still divided into classes; he still looks most
intently at the class from which he himself springs; the classes
are still so settled that he has almost forgotten that there are
classes; and he is still so secure himself that he is almost unconscious of his own position and of its security. He believes
that he is looking at the whole of life; and will always so look
at it. That is not altogether a fancy picture. Many of those
writers are still alive. Sometimes they describe their own position as young men, beginning to write, just before August 1914.
How did you learn your art? one can ask them. At College they
say—by reading; by listening; by talking. What did they talk
about? Here is Mr. Desmond MacCarthy's answer, as he gave
it, a week or two ago, in the *Sunday Times*. He was at Cambridge just before the war began and he says: "We were not
very much interested in politics. Abstract speculation was much
more absorbing; philosophy was more interesting to us than
public causes. . . . What we chiefly discussed were those 'goods'
which were ends in themselves . . . . the search for truth,

aesthetic emotions, and personal relations." In addition they read an immense amount; Latin and Greek, and of course French and English. They wrote too—but they were in no hurry to publish. They travelled;—some of them went far afield —to India, to the South Seas. But for the most part they rambled happily in the long summer holidays through England, through France, through Italy. And now and then they published books—books like Rupert Brooke's poems; novels like E. M. Forster's *Room with a View*; essays like G. K. Chesterton's essays, and reviews. It seemed to them that they were to go on living like that, and writing like that, for ever and ever. Then suddenly, like a chasm in a smooth road, the war came.

But before we go on with the story of what happened after 1914, let us look more closely for a moment, not at the writer himself, nor at his model; but at his chair. A chair is a very important part of a writer's outfit. It is the chair that gives him his attitude towards his model; that decides what he sees of human life; that profoundly affects his power of telling us what he sees. By his chair we mean his upbringing, his education. It is a fact, not a theory, that all writers from Chaucer to the present day, with so few exceptions that one hand can count them, have sat upon the same kind of chair—a raised chair. They have all come from the middle class; they have had good, at least expensive, educations. They have all been raised above the mass of people upon a tower of stucco—that is their middle-class birth; and of gold—that is their expensive education. That was true of all the nineteenth-century writers, save Dickens; it was true of all the 1914 writers, save D. H. Lawrence. Let us run through what are called "representative names": G. K. Chesterton; T. S. Eliot; Belloc; Lytton Strachey; Somerset Maugham; Hugh Walpole; Wilfred Owen; Rupert Brooke; J. E. Flecker; E. M. Forster; Aldous Huxley; G. M. Trevelyan; O. and S. Sitwell; Middleton Murry. Those are some of them; and all, with the exception of D. H. Lawrence, came of the middle class, and were educated at public schools and universities. There is another fact, equally indisputable: the books that they wrote were among the best books written between 1910 and 1925. Now let us ask, is there any connection between those facts? Is there a connection between the excellence of their work and the fact that they came of families rich enough to send them to public schools and universities?

Must we not decide, greatly though those writers differ, and shallow as we admit our knowledge of influences to be, that there must be a connection between their education and their work? It cannot be a mere chance that this minute class of educated people has produced so much that is good as writing; and that the vast mass of people without education has produced so little that is good. It is a fact, however. Take away all that the working class has given to English literature and that literature would scarcely suffer; take away all that the educated class has given, and English literature would scarcely exist. Education must then play a very important part in a writer's work.

That seems so obvious that it is astonishing how little stress has been laid upon the writer's education. It is perhaps because a writer's education is so much less definite than other educations. Reading, listening, talking, travel, leisure—many different things it seems are mixed together. Life and books must be shaken and taken in the right proportions. A boy brought up alone in a library turns into a book worm; brought up alone in the fields he turns into an earth worm. To breed the kind of butterfly a writer is you must let him sun himself for three or four years at Oxford or Cambridge—so it seems. However it is done, it is there that it is done—there that he is taught his art. And he has to be taught his art. Again, is that strange? Nobody thinks it strange if you say that a painter has to be taught his art; or a musician; or an architect. Equally a writer has to be taught. For the art of writing is at least as difficult as the other arts. And though, perhaps because the education is indefinite, people ignore this education; if you look closely you will see that almost every writer who has practised his art successfully had been taught it. He had been taught it by about eleven years of education—at private schools, public schools, and universities. He sits upon a tower raised above the rest of us; a tower built first on his parents' station, then on his parents' gold. It is a tower of the utmost importance; it decides his angle of vision; it affects his power of communication.

All through the nineteenth century, down to August 1914,

that tower was a steady tower. The writer was scarcely conscious either of his high station or of his limited vision. Many
of them had sympathy, great sympathy, with other classes;
they wished to help the working class to enjoy the advantages
of the tower class; but they did not wish to destroy the tower,
or to descend from it—rather to make it accessible to all. Nor
had the model, human life, changed essentially since Trollope
looked at it, since Hardy looked at it: and Henry James, in
1914, was still looking at it. Further, the tower itself held firm
beneath the writer during all the most impressionable years,
when he was learning his art, and receiving all those complex
influences and instructions that are summed up by the word
education. These were conditions that influenced their work
profoundly. For when the crash came in 1914 all those young
men, who were to be the representative writers of their time,
had their past, their education, safe behind them, safe within
them. They had known security; they had the memory of a
peaceful boyhood, the knowledge of a settled civilisation. Even
though the war cut into their lives, and ended some of them,
they wrote, and still write, as if the tower were firm beneath
them. In one word, they are aristocrats; the unconscious
inheritors of a great tradition. Put a page of their writing under
the magnifying-glass and you will see, far away in the distance,
the Greeks, the Romans; coming nearer, the Elizabethans;
coming nearer still, Dryden, Swift, Voltaire, Jane Austen,
Dickens, Henry James. Each, however much he differs indi-
vidually from the others, is a man of education; a man who
has learnt his art.

From that group let us pass to the next—to the group which
began to write about 1925 and, it may be, came to an end as a
group in 1939. If you read current literary journalism you will
be able to rattle off a string of names—Day Lewis, Auden,
Spender, Isherwood, Louis MacNeice and so on. They adhere
much more closely than the names of their predecessors. But
at first sight there seems little difference, in station, in education. Mr. Auden in a poem written to Mr. Isherwood says:
Behind us we have stucco suburbs and expensive educations.
They are tower dwellers like their predecessors, the sons of
well-to-do parents, who could afford to send them to public

schools and universities. But what a difference in the tower itself, in what they saw from the tower! When they looked at human life what did they see? Everywhere change; everywhere revolution. In Germany, in Russia, in Italy, in Spain, all the old hedges were being rooted up; all the old towers were being thrown to the ground. Other hedges were being planted; other towers were being raised. There was communism in one country; in another fascism. The whole of civilisation, of society, was changing. There was, it is true, neither war nor revolution in England itself. All those writers had time to write many books before 1939. But even in England towers that were built of gold and stucco were no longer steady towers. They were leaning towers. The books were written under the influence of change, under the threat of war. That perhaps is why the names adhere so closely; there was one influence that affected them all and made them, more than their predecessors, into groups. And that influence, let us remember, may well have excluded from that string of names the poets whom posterity will value most highly, either because they could not fall into step, as leaders or as followers, or because the influence was adverse to poetry, and until that influence relaxed, they could not write. But the tendency that makes it possible for us to group the names of these writers together, and gives their work a common likeness, was the tendency of the tower they sat on—the tower of middle-class birth and expensive education—to lean.

Let us imagine, to bring this home to us, that we are actually upon a leaning tower and note our sensations. Let us see whether they correspond to the tendencies we observe in those poems, plays, and novels. Directly we feel that a tower leans we become acutely conscious that we are upon a tower. All those writers too are acutely tower conscious; conscious of their middle-class birth; of their expensive educations. Then when we come to the top of the tower how strange the view looks— not altogether upside down, but slanting, sidelong. That too is characteristic of the leaning-tower writers; they do not look any class straight in the face; they look either up, or down, or sidelong. There is no class so settled that they can explore it unconsciously. That perhaps is why they create no characters. Then what do we feel next, raised in imagination on top of the tower? First discomfort; next self-pity for that discomfort; which pity soon turns to anger—to anger against the builder, against society, for making us uncomfortable. Those too seem to be tendencies of the leaning-tower writers. Discomfort; pity for themselves; anger against society. And yet—here is another tendency—how can you altogether abuse a society that is giving you, after all, a very fine view and some sort of security? You cannot abuse that society whole-heartedly while you continue to profit by that society. And so very naturally you abuse society in the person of some retired admiral or spinster or armament manufacturer; and by abusing them hope to escape whipping yourself. The bleat of the scapegoat sounds loud in their work, and the whimper of the schoolboy crying "Please, Sir, it was the other fellow, not me". Anger; pity; scapegoat beating; excuse finding—these are all very natural tendencies; if we were in their position we should tend to do the same. But we are not in their position; we have not had eleven years of expensive education. We have only been climbing an imaginary tower. We can cease to imagine. We can come down.

But they cannot. They cannot throw away their education; they cannot throw away their upbringing. Eleven years at school and college have been stamped upon them indelibly. And then, to their credit but to their confusion, the leaning tower not only leant in the thirties, but it leant more and more to the left. Do you remember what Mr. MacCarthy said about his own group at the university in 1914? "We were not very much interested in politics . . . philosophy was more interesting to us than public causes"? That shows that his tower leant neither to the right nor to the left. But in 1930 it was impossible —if you were young, sensitive, imaginative—not to be interested in politics; not to find public causes of much more pressing interest than philosophy. In 1930 young men at college were forced to be aware of what was happening in Russia; in Germany; in Italy; in Spain. They could not go on discussing aesthetic emotions and personal relations. They could not confine their reading to the poets; they had to read the politicians. They read Marx. They became communists; they became anti-fascists. The tower they realised was founded upon injustice and tyranny; it was wrong for a small class to possess an education that other people paid for; wrong to stand upon the gold that a bourgeois father had made from his bourgeois profession. It was wrong; yet how could they make it right? Their education could not be thrown away; as for their capital—did Dickens, did Tolstoy ever throw away their capital? Did D. H. Lawrence, a miner's son, continue to live like a miner? No; for it is death for a writer to throw away his capital; to be forced to earn his living in a mine or a factory. And thus, trapped by their education, pinned down by their capital, they remained on top of their leaning tower, and their state of mind as we see it reflected in their poems and plays and novels is full of discord and bitterness, full of confusion and of compromise.

These tendencies are better illustrated by quotation than by analysis. There is a poem by one of those writers, Louis MacNeice, called *Autumn Journal*. It is dated March 1939. It is feeble as poetry, but interesting as autobiography. He begins of course with a snipe at the scapegoat—the bourgeois, middle-class family from which he sprang. The retired admirals, the retired generals, and the spinster lady have breakfasted off bacon and eggs served on a silver dish, he tells us. He sketches that family as if it were already a little remote and more than a little ridiculous. But they could afford to send him to Marlborough and then to Merton, Oxford. This is what he learnt at Oxford:

> *We learned that a gentleman never misplaces his accents,*
> *That nobody knows how to speak, much less how to write*
> *English who has not hob-nobbed with the great-grandparents of*
> *English.*

Besides that he learnt at Oxford Latin and Greek; and philosophy, logic, and metaphysics:

> *Oxford* [he says] *crowded the mantelpiece with gods—*
> *Scaliger, Heinsius, Dindorf, Bentley, Wilamowitz.*

It was at Oxford that the tower began to lean. He felt that he was living under a system—

> *That gives the few at fancy prices their fancy lives*
> *While ninety-nine in the hundred who never attend the banquet*
> *Must wash the grease of ages off the knives.*

But at the same time, an Oxford education had made him fastidious:

> *It is so hard to imagine*
> *A world where the many would have their chance without*
> *A fall in the standard of intellectual living*
> *And nothing left that the highbrow cares about.*

At Oxford he got his honours degree; and that degree—in humane letters—put him in the way of a "cushy job"—seven hundred a year, to be precise, and several rooms of his own.

> *If it were not for Lit. Hum. I might be climbing*
> *A ladder with a hod,*
> *And seven hundred a year*
> *Will pay the rent and the gas and the phone and the grocer—*

And yet, again, doubts break in; the "cushy job" of teaching more Latin and Greek to more undergraduates does not satisfy him—

> *. . . the so-called humane studies*
> *May lead to cushy jobs*
> *But leave the men who land them spiritually bankrupt,*
> *Intellectual snobs.*

And what is worse, that education and that cushy job cut one off, he complains, from the common life of one's kind.

> *All that I would like to be is human, having a share*
> *In a civilised, articulate and well-adjusted*
> *Community where the mind is given its due*
> *But the body is not distrusted.*

Therefore in order to bring about that well-adjusted community he must turn from literature to politics, remembering, he says,

> *Remembering that those who by their habit*
> *Hate politics, can no longer keep their private*
> *Values unless they open the public gate*
> *To a better political system.*

So, in one way or another, he takes part in politics, and finally he ends:

> *What is it we want really?*
> *For what end and how?*
> *If it is something feasible, obtainable,*
> *Let us dream it now,*
> *And pray for a possible land*
> *Not of sleep-walkers, not of angry puppets,*
> *But where both heart and brain can understand*
> *The movements of our fellows,*
> *Where life is a choice of instruments and none*
> *Is debarred his natural music . . .*
> *Where the individual, no longer squandered*
> *In self-assertion, works with the rest . . .*

Those quotations give a fair description of the influences that have told upon the leaning-tower group. Others could easily be discovered. The influence of the films explains the lack of transitions in their work and the violently opposed contrasts. The influence of poets like Mr. Yeats and Mr. Eliot explains the obscurity. They took over from the elder poets a technique which, after many years of experiment, those poets used skilfully, and used it clumsily and often inappropriately. But we have time only to point to the most obvious influences; and these can be summed up as Leaning Tower Influences. If you think of them, that is, as people trapped on a leaning tower from which they cannot descend, much that is puzzling in their work is easier to understand It explains the violence of their attack upon bourgeois society and also its half-heartedness. They are profiting by a society which they abuse. They are flogging a dead or dying horse because a living horse, if flogged, would kick them off its back. It explains the destructiveness of their work; and also its emptiness. They can destroy bourgeois society, in part at least; but what have they put in its place? How can a writer who has no first-hand experience of a towerless, of a classless society create that society? Yet as Mr. MacNeice bears witness, they feel compelled to preach, if not by their living, at least by their writing, the creation of a society in which every one is equal and every one is free. It explains the pedagogic, the didactic, the loud speaker strain that dominates their poetry. They must teach; they must preach. Everything is a duty—even love. Listen to Mr. Day Lewis ingeminating love. "Mr. Spender," he says, "speaking from the living unit of himself and his friends appeals for the contraction of the social group to a size at which human contact may again be established and demands the destruction of all impediments to love. Listen." And we listen to this:

> *We have come at last to a country*
> *Where light, like shine from snow, strikes all faces.*
> *Here you may wonder*
> *How it was that works, money, interest, building could ever*
> *Hide the palpable and obvious love of man for man.*

We listen to oratory, not poetry. It is necessary, in order to feel the emotion of those lines, that other people should be listening too. We are in a group, in a class-room as we listen. Listen now to Wordsworth:

> *Lover had he known in huts where poor men dwell,*
> *His daily teachers had been woods and rills,*
> *The silence that is in the starry sky,*
> *The sleep that is among the lonely hills.*

We listen to that when we are alone. We remember that in solitude. Is that the difference between politician's poetry and poet's poetry? We listen to the one in company; to the other when we are alone? But the poet in the thirties was forced to be a politician. That explains why the artist in the thirties was forced to be a scapegoat. If politics were "real", the ivory tower was an escape from "reality". That explains the curious, bastard language in which so much of this leaning-tower prose and poetry is written. It is not the rich speech of the aristocrat: it is not the racy speech of the peasant. It is betwixt and between. The poet is a dweller in two worlds, one dying, the other struggling to be born. And so we come to what is perhaps the most marked tendency of leaning-tower literature—the desire to be whole; to be human. "All that I would like to be is human"—that cry rings through their books—the longing to be closer to their kind, to write the common speech of their kind, to share the emotions of their kind, no longer to be isolated and exalted in solitary state upon their tower, but to be down on the ground with the mass of human kind.

These then, briefly and from a certain angle, are some of the tendencies of the modern writer who is seated upon a leaning tower. No other generation has been exposed to them. It may be that none has had such an appallingly difficult task. Who can wonder if they have been incapable of giving us great poems, great plays, great novels? They had nothing settled to look at; nothing peaceful to remember; nothing certain to come. During all the most impressionable years of their lives they were stung into consciousness—into self-consciousness, into class-consciousness, into the consciousness of things changing, of things falling, of death perhaps about to come. There was no tranquillity in which they could recollect. The inner mind was paralysed because the surface mind was always hard at work.

Yet if they have lacked the creative power of the poet and the novelist, the power—does it come from a fusion of the two minds, the upper and the under?—that creates characters that live, poems that we all remember, they have had a power which, if literature continues, may prove to be of great value in the future. They have been great egotists. That too was forced upon them by their circumstances. When everything is rocking round one, the only person who remains comparatively stable is oneself. When all faces are changing and obscured, the only face one can see clearly is one's own. So they wrote about themselves—in their plays, in their poems, in their novels. No other ten years can have produced so much autobiography as the ten years between 1930 and 1940. No one, whatever his class or his obscurity, seems to have reached the age of thirty without writing his autobiography. But the leaning-tower writers wrote about themselves honestly, therefore creatively. They told the unpleasant truths, not only the flattering truths. That is why their autobiography is so much better than their fiction or their poetry. Consider how difficult it is to tell the truth about oneself—the unpleasant truth; to admit that one is petty, vain, mean, frustrated, tortured, unfaithful, and unsuccessful. The nineteenth-century writers never told that kind of truth, and that is why so much of the nineteenth-century writing is worthless; why, for all their genius, Dickens and Thackeray seem so often to write about dolls and puppets, not about full-grown men and women; why they are forced to evade the main themes and make do with diversions instead/ If you do not tell the truth about yourself you cannot tell it about other people. As the nineteenth century wore on, the writers knew that they were crippling themselves, diminishing their material, falsifying their object. "We are condemned", Stevenson wrote, "to avoid half the life that passes us by. What books Dickens could have written had he been permitted! Think of Thackeray as unfettered as Flaubert or Balzac! What books I might have written myself? But they give us a little box of toys and say to us 'You mustn't play with anything but these'!" Stevenson blamed society—bourgeois society was his scapegoat too. Why did he not blame himself? Why did he consent to go on playing with his little box of toys?

The leaning-tower writer has had the courage, at any rate, to throw that little box of toys out of the window. He has had the courage to tell the truth, the unpleasant truth, about himself. That is the first step towards telling the truth about other people. By analysing themselves honestly, with help from Dr. Freud, these writers have done a great deal to free us from nineteenth-century suppressions. The writers of the next generation may inherit from them a whole state of mind, a mind no longer crippled, evasive, divided. They may inherit that unconsciousness which, as we guessed—it is only a guess—at the beginning of this paper, is necessary if writers are to get beneath the surface, and to write something that people remember when they are alone. For that great gift of unconsciousness the next generation will have to thank the creative and honest egotism of the leaning-tower group.

The next generation—there will be a next generation, in spite of this war and whatever it brings. Have we time then for a rapid glance, for a hurried guess at the next generation? The next generation will be, when peace comes, a post-war generation too. Must it too be a leaning-tower generation—an oblique, sidelong, squinting, self-conscious generation with a foot in two worlds? Or will there be no more towers and no more classes and shall we stand, without hedges between us, on the common ground?

There are two reasons which lead us to think, perhaps to hope, that the world after the war will be a world without

classes or towers. Every politician who has made a speech since
September 1939 has ended with a peroration in which he has
said that we are not fighting this war for conquest; but to bring
about a new order in Europe. In that order, they tell us, we are
all to have equal opportunities, equal chances of developing
whatever gifts we may possess. That is one reason why, if they
mean what they say, and can effect it, classes and towers will
disappear. The other reason is given by the income tax. The
income tax is already doing in its own way what the politicians
are hoping to do in theirs. The income tax is saying to middle-
class parents: You cannot afford to send your sons to public
schools any longer; you must send them to the elementary
schools. One of these parents wrote to the *New Statesman* a week
or two ago. Her little boy, who was to have gone to Winchester,
had been taken away from his elementary school and sent to
the village school. "He has never been happier in his life", she
wrote. "The question of class does not arise; he is merely
interested to find how many different kinds of people there are
in the world. . . ." And she is only paying twopence-halfpenny
a week for that happiness and instruction instead of 35 guineas
a term and extras. If the pressure of the income tax continues,
classes will disappear. There will be no more upper classes;
middle classes; lower classes. All classes will be merged in one
class. How will that change affect the writer who sits at his
desk looking at human life? It will not be divided by hedges any
more. Very likely that will be the end of the novel, as we know
it. Literature, as we know it, is always ending, and beginning
again. Remove the hedges from Jane Austen's world, from
Trollope's world, and how much of their comedy and tragedy
would remain? We shall regret our Jane Austens and our
Trollopes; they gave us comedy, tragedy, and beauty. But
much of that old-class literature was very petty; very false; very
dull. Much is already unreadable. The novel of a classless and
towerless world should be a better novel than the old novel.
The novelist will have more interesting people to describe—
people who have had a chance to develop their humour, their
gifts, their tastes; real people, not people cramped and squashed
into featureless masses by hedges. The poet's gain is less obvious;
for he has been less under the dominion of hedges. But he

should gain words; when we have pooled all the different dialects, the clipped and cabined vocabulary which is all that he uses now should be enriched. Further, there might then be a common belief which he could accept, and thus shift from his shoulders the burden of didacticism, of propaganda. These then are a few reasons, hastily snatched, why we can look forward hopefully to a stronger, a more varied literature in the classless and towerless society of the future.

But it is in the future; and there is a deep gulf to be bridged between the dying world and the world that is struggling to be born. For there are still two worlds, two separate worlds. "I want", said the mother who wrote to the paper the other day about her boy, "the best of both worlds for my son." She wanted, that is, the village schoool, where he learnt to mix with the living; and the other school—Winchester it was—where he mixed with the dead. "Is he to continue", she asked, "under the system of free national education, or shall he go on—or should I say back—to the old public-school system which really is so very, very private?" She wanted the new world and the old world to unite, the world of the present and the world of the past.

But there is still a gulf between them, a dangerous gulf, in which, possibly, literature may crash and come to grief. It is easy to see that gulf; it is easy to lay the blame for it upon England. England has crammed a small aristocratic class with Latin and Greek and logic and metaphysics and mathematics until they cry out like the young men on the leaning tower, "All that I would like to be is human". She has left the other class, the immense class to which almost all of us must belong, to pick up what we can in village schools; in factories; in workshops; behind counters; and at home. When one thinks of that criminal injustice one is tempted to say England deserves to have no literature. She deserves to have nothing but detective stories, patriotic songs, and leading articles for generals, admirals, and business men to read themselves to sleep with when they are tired of winning battles and making money. But let us not be unfair; let us avoid if we can joining the embittered and futile tribe of scapegoat hunters. For some years now England has been making an effort—at last—to bridge the gulf between the two worlds. Here is one proof of that effort—this book. This book was not bought; it was not hired. It was borrowed from a public library. England lent it to a common reader, saying "It is time that even you, whom I have shut out from all my universities for centuries, should learn to read your mother tongue. I will help you." If England is going to help us, we must help her. But how? Look at what is written in the book she has lent us. "Readers are requested to point out any defects that they may observe to the local librarian." That is England's way of saying: "If I lend you books, I expect you to make yourselves critics".

We can help England very greatly to bridge the gulf between the two worlds if we borrow the books she lends us and if we read them critically. We have got to teach ourselves to understand literature. Money is no longer going to do our thinking for us. Wealth will no longer decide who shall be taught and who not. In future it is we who shall decide whom to send to public schools and universities; how they shall be taught; and whether what they write justifies their exemption from other work. In order to do that we must teach ourselves to distinguish —which is the book that is going to pay dividends of pleasure for ever; which is the book that will pay not a penny in two years' time? Try it for yourselves on new books as they come out; decide which are the lasting, which are the perishing. That is very difficult. Also we must become critics because in future we are not going to leave writing to be done for us by a small class of well-to-do young men who have only a pinch, a thimbleful of experience to give us. We are going to add our own experience, to make our own contribution. That is even more difficult. For that too we need to be critics. A writer, more than any other artist, needs to be a critic because words are so common, so familiar, that he must sieve them and sift them if they are to become enduring. Write daily; write freely; but let us always compare what we have written with what the great writers have written. It is humiliating, but it is essential. If we are going to preserve and to create, that is the only way. And we are going to do both. We need not wait till the end of the war. We can begin now. We can begin, practically and prosaically, by borrowing books from public libraries; by reading omnivorously, simultaneously, poems, plays, novels, histories, biographies, the old and the new. We must sample before we can select. It never does to be a nice feeder; each of us has an appetite that must find for itself the food that nourishes it. Nor let us shy away from the kings because we are commoners. That is a fatal crime in the eyes of Aeschylus, Shakespeare, Virgil, and Dante, who, if they could speak—and after all they can—would say, "Don't leave me to the wigged and gowned. Read me, read me for yourselves." They do not mind if we get our accents wrong, or have to read with a crib in front of us. Of course—are we not commoners, outsiders?—we shall trample many flowers and bruise much ancient grass. But let us bear in mind a piece of advice that an eminent Victorian who was also an eminent pedestrian once gave to walkers: "Whenever you see a board up with 'Trespassers will be prosecuted', trespass at once."

Let us trespass at once. Literature is no one's private ground; literature is common ground. It is not cut up into nations; there are no wars there. Let us trespass freely and fearlessly and find our own way for ourselves. It is thus that English literature will survive this war and cross the gulf—if commoners and outsiders like ourselves make that country our own country, if we teach ourselves how to read and to write, how to preserve, and how to create.

On Re-reading Novels

So there are to be new editions of Jane Austen and the Brontës and George Meredith. Left in trains, forgotten in lodging-houses, thumbed and tattered to destruction, the old ones have served their day, and for the new-comers in their new houses there are to be new editions and new readings and new friends. It speaks very well for the Georgians. It is still more to the credit of the Victorians. In spite of the mischief-makers, the grandchildren, it seems, get along very nicely with the grandparents; and the sight of their concord points inevitably to the later breach between the generations, a breach more complete than the other, and perhaps more momentous. The failure of the Edwardians, comparative yet disastrous—that is a question which waits to be discussed. How the year 1860 was a year of empty cradles; how the reign of Edward the Seventh was barren of poet, novelist, or critic; how it followed that the Georgians read Russian novels in translations; how they benefited and suffered; how different a story we might have told to-day had there been living heroes to worship and destroy—all this we find significant in view of the new editions of the old books. The Georgians, it seems, are in the odd predicament of turning for solace and guidance not to their parents who are alive, but to their grandparents who are dead. And so, as likely as not, we shall be faced one of these days by a young man reading Meredith for the first time. But before, inspired by his example, we risk the dangerous experiment of reading *Harry Richmond* for a second time, let us consider a few of the questions which the prospect of reading a long Victorian novel at once arouses in us.

First, there is the boredom of it. The national habit of reading has been formed by the drama, and the drama has always recognised the fact that human beings cannot sit for more than five hours at a stretch in front of a stage. Read *Harry Richmond* for five hours at a stretch and we shall only have broken off a fragment. Days may pass before we can add to it; meanwhile the plan is lost; the book pours to waste; we blame ourselves; we abuse the author; nothing is more exasperating and dispiriting. That is the first obstacle to be overcome. Next, we cannot doubt that we are by temperament and tradition poetic. There still lingers among us the belief that poetry is the senior branch of the service. If we have an hour to spend, we feel that we lay it out to better advantage with Keats than with Macaulay. Novels, however, besides being so long and so badly written, are all about the old familiar things; what we do, week in, week out, between breakfast and bedtime; they are about life, and one has life enough on one's hands already without living it all over again in prose.

That is another obstacle. Yet these stock complaints which we begin to hear and, perhaps, to utter (as we get on in life) lose nothing of their acrimony if with the same breath we have to admit that we owe more to Tolstoy, Flaubert, and Hardy than we can measure; that if we wish to recall our happier hours, they would be those Conrad has given us and Henry James; and that to have seen a young man bolting Meredith whole recalls the pleasure of so many first readings that we are even ready to venture a second. The question is whether, if we venture ourselves a second time with *Vanity Fair*, the Copperfields, the Richmonds, we shall be able to find some other form of pleasure to take the place of that careless rapture which floated us along so triumphantly in the first instance. The pleasure we shall now look for will lie not so obviously on the surface; and we shall find ourselves hard pressed to make out what is the lasting quality, if such there be, which justifies these long books about modern life in prose.

Some months ago Mr. Percy Lubbock applied himself to answer some of these questions in *The Craft of Fiction*, a book which is likely to have much influence upon readers and may perhaps eventually reach the critics and the writers. The subject is vast and the book short; but it will be our fault, not Mr. Lubbock's, if we talk as vaguely about novels in the future as we have done in the past. For example, do we say that we cannot read *Harry Richmond* twice? We are led by Mr. Lubbock to suspect that it was our first reading that was to blame. A strong but vague emotion, two or three characters, half a dozen scattered scenes—if that is all that *Harry Richmond* recalls to us, the fault lies perhaps not with Meredith, but with ourselves. Did we read the book as he meant it to be read, or did we not reduce it to chaos through our own incompetency? Novels, above all other books, we are reminded, bristle with temptations. We identify ourselves with this person or with that. We fasten upon the character or the scene which is congenial. We swing our imaginations capriciously from spot to spot. We compare the world of fiction with the real world and judge it by the same standards. Undoubtedly we do all this and easily find excuses for so doing. "But meanwhile the book, the thing he made, lies imprisoned in the volume, and our glimpse of it was too fleeting, it seems, to leave us with a lasting knowledge of its form." That is the point. There is something lasting that we can know, something solid that we can lay hands on. There is, Mr. Lubbock argues, such a thing as the book itself. To perceive this we should read at arm's length from the distractions we have named. We must receive impressions but we must relate them to each other as the author intended. And it is when we have shaped our impressions as the author intended that we are then in a position to perceive the form itself, and it is this which endures, however mood or fashion may change. In Mr. Lubbock's own words:

> But with the book in this condition of a defined shape, firm of outline, its form shows for what it is indeed—not an attribute, one of many and possibly not the most important, but the book itself, as the form of the statue is the statue itself.

Now, as Mr. Lubbock laments, the criticism of fiction is in its infancy, and its language, though not all of one syllable, is baby language. This word "form", of course, comes from the visual arts, and for our part we wish that he could have seen his way to do without it. It is confusing. The form of the novel differs from the dramatic form—that is true; we can, if we choose, say that we see the difference in our mind's eyes. But can we see that the form of *The Egoist* differs from the form of *Vanity Fair*? We do not raise the question in order to stickle for

accuracy where most words are provisional, many meta-
phorical, and some on trial for the first time. The question is
not one of words only. It goes deeper than that, into the very
process of reading itself. Here we have Mr. Lubbock telling us
that the book itself is equivalent to its form, and seeking with
admirable subtlety and lucidity to trace out those methods by
which novelists build up the final and enduring structure of
their books. The very patness with which the image comes to
the pen makes us suspect that it fits a little loosely. And in these
circumstances it is best to shake oneself free from images and
start afresh with a definite subject to work upon. Let us read a
story and set down our impressions as we go along, and so perhaps discover what it is that bothers us in Mr. Lubbock's use
of the word form. For this purpose there is no more appropriate
author than Flaubert; and, not to strain our space, let us
choose a short story, *Un Cœur Simple*, for example, for, as it
happens, it is one that we have practically forgotten.

The title gives us our bearings, and the first words direct our
attention to Madame Aubain's faithful servant Félicité. And
now the impressions begin to arrive. Madame's character; the
look of her house; Félicité's appearance; her love affair with
Théodore; Madame's children; her visitors; the angy bull. We
accept them, but we do not use them. We lay them aside in
reserve. Our attention flickers this way and that, from one to
another. Still the impressions accumulate, and still, almost
ignoring their individual quality, we read on, noting the pity,
the irony, hastily observing certain relations and contrasts, but
stressing nothing; always awaiting the final signal. Suddenly
we have it. The mistress and the maid are turning over
the dead child's clothes. "Et des papillons s'envolèrent de
l'armoire." The mistress kisses the servant for the first time.
"Félicité lui en fut reconnaissante comme d'un bienfait, et
désormais la chérit avec un dévouement bestial et une vénéra-
tion religieuse." A sudden intensity of phrase, something which
for good reasons or for bad we feel to be emphatic, startles us
into a flash of understanding. We see now why the story was
written. Later in the same way we are roused by a sentence
with a very different intention: "Et Félicité priait en regardant
l'image, mais de temps à autre se tournait un peu vers l'oiseau."

Again we have the same conviction that we know why the story was written. And then it is finished. All the observations which we have put aside now come out and range themselves according to the directions we have received. Some are relevant; others we can find no place for. On a second reading we are able to use our observations from the start, and they are much more precise; but they are still controlled by these moments of understanding.

Therefore the "book itself" is not form which you see, but emotion which you feel, and the more intense the writer's feeling the more exact without slip or chink its expression in words. And whenever Mr. Lubbock talks of form it is as if something were interposed between us and the book as we know it. We feel the presence of an alien substance which requires to be visualised imposing itself upon emotions which we feel naturally, and name simply, and range in final order by feeling their right relations to each other. Thus we have reached our conception of *Un Cœur Simple* by working from the emotion outwards, and, the reading over, there is nothing to be seen; there is everything to be felt. And only when the emotion is feeble and the workmanship excellent can we separate what is felt from the expression and remark, for example, what excellence of form *Esther Waters* possesses in comparison with *Jane Eyre*. But consider the *Princesse de Clèves*. There is vision and there is expression. The two blend so perfectly that when Mr. Lubbock asks us to test the form with our eyes we see nothing at all. But we feel with singular satisfaction, and since all our feelings are in keeping, they form a whole which remains in our minds as the book itself. The point is worth labouring, not simply to substitute one word for another, but to insist, among all this talk of methods, that both in writing and in reading it is the emotion that must come first.

Still, we have only made a beginning and a very dangerous one at that. To snatch an emotion and luxuriate in it and tire of it and throw it away is as dissipating in literature as in life. Yet if we wring this pleasure from Flaubert, the most austere of writers, there is no limit to be put upon the intoxicating effects of Meredith and Dickens and Dostoevsky and Scott and Charlotte Brontë. Or rather there is a limit, and we have found

it over and over again in the extremes of satiety and disillusion-
ment. If we are to read them again we must somehow dis-
criminate. Emotion is our material; but what value do we put
on the emotion? How many different kinds of emotion are
there not in one short story, of how many qualities, and composed of how many different elements? And therefore to get
our emotion directly and for ourselves is only the first step.
We must go on to test it and riddle it with questions. If nothing
survives, well and good; toss it into the waste-paper basket and
have done with it. If something survives, place it for ever among
the treasures of the universe. Is there not something beyond
emotion, something which though it is inspired by emotion,
tranquillises it, orders it, composes it?—that which Mr. Lubbock
calls form, which, for simplicity's sake, we will call art? Can
we not discover even in the vortex and whirlpool of Victorian
fiction some constraint which the most ebullient of novelists
forced himself to lay on his material, to reduce it to symmetry?
Of a playwright it would scarcely be necessary to ask so simple-
minded a question. The most casual visitor to the theatre must
instantly perceive how straitly even the crudest drama is
shepherded by conventions; and can bring to mind subtler
instances of dramatic technique which have been in force and
have obtained recognition these many hundred years. In
Macbeth, for instance, critic after critic points out the effect of
change from tragedy to comedy in the scene of the porter; and
in the *Antigone* of Sophocles we are bidden to remark how the
messenger rearranges the story so as make the discovery of
the death of Antigone succeed, instead of preceding, the
funeral.

The drama, however, is hundreds of years in advance of the
novel. We must have known that a novelist, before he can
persuade us that his world is real and his people alive, before
he can begin to move us by the sight of their joys and sufferings,
must solve certain questions and acquire certain skill. But so far
we have swallowed our fiction with our eyes shut. We have not
named and therefore presumably not recognised the simplest of
devices by which every novel has to come into being. We have
not taken the pains to watch our story-teller as he decides
which method he will use; we have not applauded his choice,

deplored his lack of judgment, or followed with delight and interest his use of some dangerous new device which, for all we know, may do his job to perfection or blow the whole book to smithereens.

In excuse of our slovenliness it must be admitted, not only that the methods are unnamed, but that no writer has so many at his disposal as a novelist. He can put himself at any point of view; he can to some extent combine several different views. He can appear in person, like Thackeray; or disappear (never perhaps completely), like Flaubert. He can state the facts, like Defoe, or give the thought without the fact, like Henry James. He can sweep the widest horizons, like Tolstoy, or seize upon one old apple-woman and her basket, like Tolstoy again. Where there is every freedom there is every licence; and the novel, open-armed, free to all comers, claims more victims than the other forms of literature all put together. But let us look at the victors. We are tempted, indeed, to look at them a great deal more closely than space allows. For they too look different if you watch them at work. There is Thackeray always taking measures to avoid a scene, and Dickens (save in *David Copperfield*) invariably seeking one. There is Tolstoy dashing into the midst of his story without staying to lay foundations, and Balzac laying foundations so deep that the story itself seems never to begin. But we must check the desire to see where Mr. Lubbock's criticism would lead us in reading particular books. The general view is more striking and a general view is to be had.

Let us look, not at each story separately, but at the method of telling stories as a whole, and its development from generation to generation. Let us look at it in Richardson's hands, and watch it changing and developing as Thackeray applies it, and Dickens and Tolstoy and Meredith and Flaubert and the rest. Then let us see how in the end Henry James, endowed not with greater genius but with greater knowledge and craftsmanship, surmounts in *The Ambassadors* problems which baffled Richardson in *Clarissa*. The view is difficult; the light is bad. At every angle some one rises to protest that novels are the outburst of spontaneous inspiration, and that Henry James lost as much by his devotion to art as he gained. We will not silence that protest, for it is the voice of an immediate joy in reading without which second readings would be impossible, for there would be no first. And yet the conclusion seems to us undeniable, Henry James achieved what Richardson attempted. "The only real *scholar* in the art" beats the amateurs. The latecomer improves upon the pioneers. More is implied than we can even attempt to state.

For from that vantage ground the art of fiction can be seen, not clearly indeed, but in a new proportion. We may speak of infancy, of youth, and of maturity. We may say that Scott is childish and Flaubert by comparison a grown man. We may go on to say that the vigour and splendour of youth almost outweigh the more deliberate virtues of maturity. And then we may pause upon the significance of "almost", and wonder whether, perhaps, it has not some bearing upon our reluctance to read the Victorians twice. The gigantic, sprawling books still seem to reverberate the yawns and lamentations of their makers. To build a castle, sketch a profile, fire off a poem, reform a workhouse, or pull down a prison were occupations more congenial to the writers, or more befitting their manhood, than to sit chained at a desk scribbling novels for a simple-minded public. The genius of Victorian fiction seems to be making its magnificent best of an essentially bad job. But it is never possible to say of Henry James that he is making the best of a bad job. In all the long stretch of *The Wings of the Dove* and *The Ambassadors* there is not the hint of a yawn, not a sign of condescension. The novel is his job. It is the appropriate form for what he has to say. It wins a beauty from that fact—a fine and noble beauty which it has never worn before. And now at last it has worked itself free and made itself distinct from its companions. It will not burden itself with other people's relics. It will choose to say whatever it says best. Flaubert will take for his subject an old maid and a stuffed parrot. Henry James will find all he needs round a tea-table in a drawing-room. The nightingales and roses are banished—or at least the nightingale sounds strange against the traffic, and the roses in the light of the arc lamps are not quite so red. There are new combinations of old material, and the novel, when it is used for the sake of its qualities and not for the sake of its defects, enforces fresh aspects of the perennial story.

Mr. Lubbock prudently carries his survey no further than the novels of Henry James. But already the years have mounted up. We may expect the novel to change and develop as it is explored by the most vigorous minds of a very complex age. What have we not, indeed, to expect from M. Proust alone? But if he will listen to Mr. Lubbock, the common reader will refuse to sit any longer open-mouthed in passive expectation. That is to encourage the charlatan to shock us and the conjuror to play us tricks.

From all this some conclusions seem to emerge. First, that when we speak of form we mean that certain emotions have been placed in the right relations to each other; then that the novelist is able to dispose these emotions and make them tell by methods which he inherits, bends to his purpose, models anew, or even invents for himself. Further, that the reader can detect these devices, and by so doing will deepen his understanding of the book, while, for the rest, it may be expected that novels will lose their chaos and become more and more shapely as the novelist explores and perfects his technique. Finally, perhaps, a charge is laid upon the indolence and credulity of the reader. Let him press hard upon the novelist's heels; be quick to follow, quick to understand, and so bring to bear upon him, even in his study, with reams of paper at his disposal and publishers eager to accept the bloated productions of his solitude, the chastening and salutary pressure which a dramatist has to reckon with, from actors, the spectators, and the audience trained for generations in the art of going to the play.

Personalities

"I MUST have Keats's 'Love Letters' out; though I confess there is something in the personality of Keats, some sort of semi-physical aroma wafted from it, which I cannot endure." Such was the opinion of J. A. Symonds—one highly unfashionable at the present moment, and, apart from that circumstance, sufficiently remarkable in itself. For most people will exclaim that if ever there was a lovable human being, one whom one would wish to live with, walk with, go on foreign travels with, it was Keats. He was rather below middle height; his shoulders were perhaps a little broad for his size; his eyes glowed with inspiration, but at the same time expressed the greatest consideration for the feelings of others. He was vigorous but gentle in all his movements, wearing neat black shoes, trousers strapped under his insteps, and a coat that was a little shabby at the seams. His eyes were of a warm yet searching brown, his hands were broad, and the fingers, unlike those of most artists, square at the tip. So we could go on making it up, page after page, whether accurately or not does not for our present purpose very much matter. For the point we wish to make is that we are ready supplied with a picture of Keats, and have the same liking or disliking for him personally that we have for a friend last seen half an hour ago in the corner of the omnibus that plies between Holborn and Ludgate Hill. Symonds also received an impression of extreme vividness, though of a distasteful kind; and both our impressions, though they affect our feelings for the poetry, are not directly caused by it, though from what they rise it would be hard to say. "What a curious thing is that undefinable flavour of personality," Symonds continues, "suggestion of physical quality, odour of the man in his unconscious and spontaneous self-determination, which attracts or repels so powerfully, and is at the very root of love or dislike." How much of it, we go on to consider, enters into our feelings for books, and how difficult it is to be certain that

135

a sense of the physical presence of the writer, with all which that implies, is not colouring our judgment of his work. Yet the critics tell us that we should be impersonal when we write, and therefore impersonal when we read. Perhaps that is true, and it may be that the greatest passages in literature have about them something of the impersonality which belongs to our own emotions at their strongest. The great poet and the lover are both representative—in some way anonymous. But these are high matters. My purpose in dwelling upon this old-fashioned view of Keats is to confess similar prejudices, partly as an act of atonement for critical malpractices, and partly in order to see whether, when they are set out, any sense can be made of them.

It seems to me possible that our attitude to Greek literature, so queer in its reverence, servility, boredom, querulousness, and uneasiness, may be due to the fact that we have either no sense or a very weak one of the personality of the Greek dramatists. The scholars may contradict this. To them Aeschylus may be as real as a man in an omnibus—as real as Keats himself; but if that is so they have been singularly unsuccessful in impressing what they feel upon the popular imagination. I shut my eyes and summon Aeschylus before me, and all I see is a venerable old man wrapped in a blanket sitting on a marble plinth in the sun. An eagle soars high in the blue. Suddenly from his beak drops a large stone. It catches Aeschylus on the back of the head, splits his skull open, and that is all. Similarly with Sappho—she leapt from a high rock into the sea. Both anecdotes have something barren and academical about them, something detached and unilluminating. If we transpose them to our own day and imagine Tennyson killed on the steps of St. Paul's by an escaped eagle—but that is too fantastic—let us suppose him run over by a taxi cab; or George Eliot gathering her skirts about her and leaping from a cliff, the difference between our attitude to Greek and our attitude to English literature is at once apparent. If these catastrophes had happened to our great writers, we should know a multitude of additional facts—how it happened, what they said, wore, and looked like; libraries of comment and psychology would have been spun from them, and it is through that veil that we should have been forced to read *In Memoriam* and *Middlemarch*. It cannot be denied that the Greeks have a pull over us in this as in other respects. The ordinary reader resents the bareness of their literature. There is nothing in the way of anecdote to browse upon, nothing handy and personal to help oneself up by; nothing is left but the literature itself, cut off from us by time and language, unvulgarised by association, pure from contamination, but steep and isolated. That is a happy fate for a literature, if it did not follow that very few people read it and that those who do become a little priest-like—inevitably solitary and pure, reading with more ingenuity but with less humanity than the ordinary person, and thus leaving out something—is it the character, the personality "which is at the very root of love and dislike"—which we guess to be there, but which, save for glimpses, we can never find for ourselves. We are intolerably exacting. A few patient scholars, shut up in their studies—what can they do for us? Perhaps one must read collectively, learned side by side with the unlearned, for generations, as we have read Shakespeare, to work through to that kind of contact.

But directly Shakespeare is mentioned there comes to mind the popular opinion that he, of all great men, is the least familiar. Indeed very little is known of him biographically, but it is evident that most people have precisely that personal feeling for him which I think they have not for Aeschylus. There is never an essay upon Hamlet which does not make out with some confidence the author's view of what he calls "Shakespeare the man". Yet Shakespeare is a very queer case. Undoubtedly one has the certainty of knowing him; but it is as fleeting as it is intense. You think you have fixed him for ever; you look again, and something seems withheld. All your preconceptions are falsified. What was Shakespeare may, after all, have been Hamlet; or yourself; or poetry. These great artists who manage to infuse the whole of themselves into their works, yet contrive to universalise their identity so that, though we feel Shakespeare everywhere about, we cannot catch him at the moment in any particular spot. But it is simpler to take a much smaller example of the same quality. There is Jane Austen, thumbed, scored, annotated, magnified, living almost within the memory of man, and yet as inscrutable in her small way as

Shakespeare in his vast one. She flatters and cajoles you with the promise of intimacy and then, at the last moment, there is the same blankness. Are those Jane Austen's eyes or is it a glass, a mirror, a silver spoon held up in the sun? The people whom we admire most as writers, then, have something elusive, enigmatic, impersonal about them. They rise slowly to their heights; and there they shine. They do not win fame directly, nor are they exposed to the alternations of praise and blame which rise from the passions and prejudices of our hearts. In ransacking their drawers we shall find out little about them. All has been distilled into their books. The life is thin, modest, colourless, like blue skimmed milk at the bottom of the jar. It is the imperfect artists who never manage to say the whole thing in their books who wield the power of personality over us.

This would be all very well if we could make it square with the facts, but unfortunately with Keats as an example of the kind of writer whose personality affects us we can do no such thing. We must then go humbly and confess that our likings and dislikings for authors in their books are as varied and as little accountable as our likings for people in the flesh. Some show themselves, others hide themselves, irrespective of their greatness. Here is Jane Austen, a great writer as we all agree, but, for my own part, I would rather not find myself alone in the room with her. A sense of meaning withheld, a smile at something unseen, an atmosphere of perfect control and courtesy mixed with something finely satirical, which, were it not directed against things in general rather than against individuals, would be almost malicious, would, so I feel, make it alarming to find her at home. On the other hand Charlotte Brontë, so easily stirred by timely mention of the Duke of Wellington, so vehement, irrational, and caustic, would be far easier to know, easier, it seems to me, to love. Her very faults make a breach through which one steps into intimacy. It is the fact that one likes people in spite of their faults, and then likes the faults because they are theirs, that makes one distrust criticism, and wake, after attempting it, in horror at dead of night. It will be remembered that Charlotte Brontë made herself ridiculous when she introduced a Baroness and a footman into the pages of *Jane Eyre*. Mrs. Humphry Ward points out the absurdity of the scene; and into what bottomless pit of iniquity do we not drop Mrs. Humphry Ward eternally for that very just observation? Again, no one has written worse English than Mr. Hardy in some of his novels—cumbrous, stilted, ugly, and inexpressive—yes, but at the same time so strangely expressive of something attractive to us in Mr. Hardy himself that we would not change it for the perfection of Sterne at his best. It becomes coloured by its surroundings; it becomes literature. These are the passages that admirers tend to imitate; and when untinged by his character one sees clearly enough how bad they are. But we need not apologise for injustice to writers of this calibre. It is when we find ourselves swayed by passion in judging the work of contemporaries that we must be on our guard. How we, who cannot hold the reader's attention and maunder on through chapter after chapter of colourless disquisition, yet contrive to impress him with such a distaste for our personality that he bristles at the mere mention of our names, I know not. But it is a fact. The legacy of a negligible novel is often an oddly vivid sense of the writer's character, a fancy sketch of his circumstances, a disposition to like or dislike which works its way into the text and possibly falsifies its meaning. Or do we only read with all our faculties when we seize this impression too?

Pictures

Probably some professor has written a book on the subject, but it has not come our way. "The Loves of the Arts"—that is more or less the title it would bear, and it would be concerned with the flirtations between music, letters, sculpture, and architecture, and the effects that the arts have had upon each other throughout the ages. Pending his inquiry it would seem on the face of it that literature has always been the most sociable and the most impressionable of them all; that sculpture influenced Greek literature, music Elizabethan, architecture the English of the eighteenth century, and now undoubtedly we are under the dominion of painting. Were all modern paintings to be destroyed, a critic of the twenty-fifth century would be able to deduce from the works of Proust alone the existence of Matisse, Cézanne, Derain, and Picasso; he would be able to say with those books before him that painters of the highest originality and power must be covering canvas after canvas, squeezing tube after tube, in the room next door.

Yet it is extremely difficult to put one's finger on the precise spot where paint makes itself felt in the work of so complete a writer. In the partial and incomplete writers it is much easier to detect. The world is full of cripples at the moment, victims of the art of painting who paint apples, roses, china, pomegranates, tamarinds, and glass jars as well as words can paint them, which is, of course, not very well. We can say for certain that a writer whose writing appeals mainly to the eye is a bad writer; that if in describing, say, a meeting in a garden he describes roses, lilies, carnations, and shadows on the grass, so that we can see them, but allows to be inferred from them ideas, motives, impulses, and emotions, it is that he is incapable of using his medium for the purposes for which it was created, and is as a writer a man without legs.

But it is impossible to bring that charge against Proust,

Written in 1925

Hardy, Flaubert, or Conrad. They are using their eyes without in the least impeding their pens, and they are using them as novelists have never used them before. Moors and woods, tropical seas, ships, harbours, streets, drawing-rooms, flowers, clothes, attitudes, effects of light and shade—all this they have given us with an accuracy and a subtlety that make us exclaim that now at last writers have begun to use their eyes. Not indeed that any of these great writers stops for a moment to describe a crystal jar as if it were an end in itself; the jars on their mantel-pieces are always seen through the eyes of women in the room. The whole scene, however solidly and pictorially built up, is always dominated by an emotion which has nothing to do with the eye. But it is the eye that has fertilised their thought; it is the eye, in Proust above all, that has come to the help of the other senses, combined with them, and produced effects of extreme beauty, and of a subtlety hitherto unknown. Here is a scene in a theatre, for example. We have to understand the emotions of a young man for a lady in a box below. With an abundance of images and comparisons we are made to appreci-ate the forms, the colours, the very fibre and texture of the plush seats and the ladies' dresses and the dullness or glow, sparkle or colour, of the light. At the same time that our senses drink in all this our minds are tunnelling logically and intel-lectually into the obscurity of the young man's emotions, which as they ramify and modulate and stretch further and further, at last penetrate too far, peter out into such a shred of meaning that we can scarcely follow any more, were it not that suddenly in flash after flash, metaphor after metaphor, the eye lights up that cave of darkness and we are shown the hard tangible material shapes of bodiless thoughts hanging like bats in the primeval darkness where light has never visited them before.

A writer thus has need of a third eye whose function it is to help out the other senses when they flag. But it is extremely doubtful whether he learns anything directly from painting. Indeed it would seem to be true that writers are, of all critics of painting, the worst—the most prejudiced, the most distorted in their judgments; if we accost them in picture galleries, dis-arm their suspicions and get them to tell us honestly what it is that pleases them in pictures, they will confess that it is not the art of painting in the least. They are not there to understand the problems of the painter's art. They are after something that may be helpful to themselves. It is only thus that they can turn those long galleries from torture chambers of boredom and despair into smiling avenues, pleasant places filled with birds, sanctuaries where silence reigns supreme. Free to go their own way, to pick and choose at their will, they find moden pictures, they say, very helpful, very stimulating. Cézanne, for example —no painter is more provocative to the literary sense, because his pictures are so audaciously and provocatively content to be paint that the very pigment, they say, seems to challenge us, to press on some nerve, to stimulate, to excite. That picture, for example, they explain (standing before a rocky landscape all cleft in ridges of opal colour as if by a giant's hammer, silent, solid, serene), stirs words in us where we had not thought words to exist; suggests forms where we had never seen anything but thin air. As we gaze, words begin to raise their feeble limbs in the pale border-land of no man's language, to sink down again in despair. We fling them like nets upon a rocky and inhospitable shore; they fade and disappear. It is vain, it is futile; but we can never resist the temptation. The silent painters, Cézanne and Mr. Sickert, make fools of us as often as they choose.

But painters lose their power directly they attempt to speak. They must say what they have to say by shading greens into blues, posing block upon block. They must weave their spells like mackerel behind the glass at the aquarium, mutely, mysteriously. Once let them raise the glass and begin to speak, and the spell is broken. A story-telling picture is as pathetic and ludicrous as a trick played by a dog, and we applaud it only because we know that it is as hard for a painter to tell a story with his brush as it is for a sheep-dog to balance a biscuit on its nose. Dr. Johnson at the Mitre is much better told by Boswell; in paint, Keats's nightingale is dumb; with half a sheet of note-paper we can tell all the stories of all the pictures in the world.

Nevertheless, they admit, moving round the gallery, even when they do not tempt us to the heroic efforts which have produced so many abortive monsters, pictures are very pleasant things. There is a great deal to be learned from them. That picture of a wet marsh on a blowing day shows us much more clearly than we could see for ourselves the greens and silvers, the sliding streams, the gusty willows shivering in the wind, and sets us trying to find phrases for them, suggests even a figure lying there among the bulrushes, or coming out of the farm-yard gate in top-boots and mackintosh. That still-life, they proceed, pointing to a jar of red-hot pokers, is to us what a beefsteak is to an invalid—an orgy of blood and nourishment, so starved we are on our diet of thin black print. We nestle into its colour, feed and fill ourselves with yellow and red and gold till we drop off, nourished and content. Our sense of colour seems miraculously sharpened. We carry those roses and red-hot pokers about with us for days, working them over again in words. From a portrait, too, we get almost always something worth having—somebody's room, nose, or hands, some little effect of character or circumstance, some knick-knack to put in our pockets and take away. But again, the portrait painter must not attempt to speak; he must not say "This is maternity; that intellect", the utmost he must do is to tap on the wall of the room, or the glass of the aquarium; he must come very close, but something must always separate us from him.

There are artists, indeed, who are born tappers; no sooner do we see a picture of a dancer tying up her shoe by Degas than we exclaim "How witty!" exactly as if we had read a speech by Congreve. Degas detaches a scene and comments upon it exactly as a great comic writer detaches and comments, but silently, without for a moment infringing the reticences of paint. We laugh, but not with the muscles that laugh in read-ing. Mlle Lessore has the same rare and curious power. How witty her circus horses are, or her groups standing with field-glasses gazing, or her fiddlers in the pit of the orchestra! How she quickens our sense of the point and gaiety of life by tapping on the other side of the wall! Matisse taps, Derain taps, Mr. Grant taps; Picasso, Sickert, Mrs. Bell, on the other hand, are all mute as mackerel.

But the writers have said enough. Their consciences are un-easy. No one knows better than they do, they murmur, that this is not the way to look at pictures; that they are irresponsible dragon-flies, mere insects, children wantonly destroying works of art by pulling petal from petal. In short, they had better be off, for here, oaring his way through the waters, mooning, abstract, contemplative, comes a painter, and stuffing their pilferings into their pockets, out they bolt, lest they should be caught at their mischief and made to suffer the most extreme of penalties, the most exquisite of tortures—to be made to look at pictures with a painter.

Harriette Wilson

ACROSS the broad continent of a woman's life falls the shadow of a sword. On one side all is correct, definite, orderly; the paths are strait, the trees regular, the sun shaded; escorted by gentlemen, protected by policemen, wedded and buried by clergymen, she has only to walk demurely from cradle to grave and no one will touch a hair of her head. But on the other side all is confusion. Nothing follows a regular course. The paths wind between bogs and precipices. The trees roar and rock and fall in ruin. There, too, what strange company is to be met—in what bewildering variety! Stone-masons hobnob with Dukes of the blood royal—Mr. Blore treads on the heels of His Grace the Duke of Argyll. Byron rambles through, the Duke of Wellington marches in with all his orders on him. For in that strange land gentlemen are immune; any being of the male sex can cross from sun to shade with perfect safety. In that strange land money is poured out lavishly; bank-notes drop on to breakfast plates; pearl rings are found beneath pillows; champagne flows in fountains; but over it all broods the fever of a nightmare and the transiency of a dream. The brilliant fade; the great mysteriously disappear; the diamonds turn to cinders, and the Queens are left sitting on three-legged stools shivering in the cold. That great Princess, Harriette Wilson, with her box at the Opera and the Peerage at her feet, found herself before she was fifty reduced to solitude, to poverty, to life in foreign parts, to marriage with a Colonel, to scribbling for cash whatever she could remember or invent of her past.

Nevertheless it would be a grave mistake to think that Harriette repented her ways or would have chosen another career had she had the chance. She was a girl of fifteen when she stepped across the sword and became, for reasons which she will not specify, the mistress of the Earl of Craven. A few facts leak out later. She was educated at a convent and shocked the

Written in 1925

nuns. Her parents had fifteen children; their home was "truly uncomfortable"; her father was a Swiss with a passion for mathematics, always on the point of solving a problem, and furious if interrupted; while the unhappiness of her parents' married life had decided Harriette before she was ten "to live free as air from any restraint but that of my own conscience". So she stepped across. And at once, the instant her foot touched those shifting sands, everything wobbled; her character, her principles, the world itself—all suffered a sea change. For ever after (it is one of the curiosities of her memoirs—one of the obstacles to any certain knowledge of her character) she is outside the pale of ordinary values and must protest till she is black in the face, and run up a whole fabric of lies into the bargain, before she can make good her claim to a share in the emotions of human kind. Could an abandoned woman love a sister, could a mere prostitute grieve genuinely for a mother's death? Mr. Thomas Seccombe, in the *Dictionary of National Biography*, had his doubts. Harriette Wilson, he said, described her sister's death "with an appearance of feeling", whereas to Mr. Seccombe Lord Hertford's kindness in soothing the same creature's last hours was indisputably genuine.

Outcast as she was, her position had another and an incongruous result. She was impelled, though nothing was further from her liking than serious thought, to speculate a little curiously about the law of society, to consult, with odd results, the verdict of "my own conscience". For example, the marriage-law—was that as impeccably moral as people made out? "I cannot for the life of me divest myself of the idea that if all were alike honourable and true, as I wish to be, it would be unnecessary to bind men and women together by law, since two persons who may have chosen each other from affection, possessing heart and honour, could not part, and where there is neither the one nor the other, even marriage does not bind. My idea may be wicked or erroneous," she adds hastily, for what could be more absurd than that Harriette Wilson should set herself up as a judge of morality—Harry, as the gentlemen called her, whose only rule of conduct was "One wants a little variety in life", who left one man because he bored her, and another because he drew pictures of cocoa-trees on vellum

paper, and seduced poor young Lord Worcester, and went off
to Melton Mowbray with Mr. Meyler, and, in short, was the
mistress of any man who had money and rank and a person
that took her fancy? No, Harriette was not moral, nor refined,
nor, it appears, very beautiful, but merely a bustling bouncing
vivacious creature with good eyes and dark hair and "the
manners of a wild schoolboy", said Sir Walter Scott, who had
dined in her presence. But it cannot be doubted—otherwise her
triumph is inexplicable—that gifts she had, gifts of dash and
go and enthusiasm, which still stir among the dead leaves of her
memoirs and impart even to their rambling verbosity and
archness and vulgarity some thrill of that old impetuosity, some
flash of those fine dark eyes, some fling of those wild schoolboy
manners which, when furbished up in plumes and red plush
and diamonds, held our ancestors enthralled.

She was, of course, always falling in love. She saw a stranger
riding with a Newfoundland dog in Knightsbridge and lost her
heart to his "pale expressive beauty" at once. She venerated
his door-knocker even, and when Lord Ponsonby—for Lord
Ponsonby it was—deserted her, she flung herself sobbing on a
doorstep in Half Moon Street and was carried, raving and
almost dying, back to bed. Large and voluptuous herself,
she loved for the most part little men with small hands and
feet, and, like Mr. Meyler, skins of remarkable transparency,
"churchyard skins", foreboding perhaps an early death; "yet it
would be hard to die, in the bloom of youth and beauty,
beloved by everybody, and with thirty thousand a year". She
loved, too, the Apollo Belvedere, and sat entranced at the
Louvre, exclaiming in ecstasy at the "quivering lips—the
throat!", till it seemed as if she must share the fate of another
lady who sat by the Apollo, "whom she could not warm, till
she went raving mad, and in that state died". But it is not her
loves that distinguish her; her passions tend to become perfunctory; her young men with fine skins and large fortunes
innumerable; her rhapsodies and recriminations monotonous.
It is when off duty, released from the necessity of painting the
usual picture in the usual way, that she becomes capable of
drawing one of those pictures which only seem to await some
final stroke to become a page in *Vanity Fair* or a sketch by

Hogarth. All the materials of comedy seem heaped in disorder before us as she, the most notorious woman in London, retires to Charmouth to await the return of her lover, Lord Worcester, from the Spanish wars, trots to church on the arm of the curate's aged father, or peeps from her window at the rustic beauties of Lyme Regis tripping down to the sixpenny Assembly Rooms with "turbans or artificial flowers twined around their wigs" to dance at five in the evening on the shores of the innocent sea. So a famous prima donna, hidden behind a curtain in strict incognito, might listen to country girls singing a rustic ballad with contempt and amusement, and a dash of envy too, for how simply the good people accepted her. Harriette could not help reflecting how kindly they sympathised with her anxiety about her husband at the wars, and sat up with her to watch for the light of the postwoman's lanthorn as she came late at night over the hill from Lyme Regis with letters from Mr. Wilson in Spain! All she could do to show her gratitude was to pay twice what they asked her, to shower clothes upon ragged children, to mend a poor country-woman's roof, and then, tired of the role of Lady Bountiful, she was off to join Lord Worcester in Spain.

Now, for a moment, before the old story is resumed, sketched with a stump of rapid charcoal, springs into existence, to fade for ever after, the figure of Miss Martha Edmonds, her land-lady's sister. "I am old enough," exclaimed the gallant old maid, "and thank God I am no beauty. . . . I have never yet been ten miles from my native place, and I want to see the world." She declared her intention of escorting Mrs. Wilson to Falmouth; she had her ancient habit made up for the purpose. Off they started, the old maid and the famous courtesan, to starve and freeze in an upper room of a crowded Falmouth inn, the winds being adverse, until in some mysterious way Mrs. Wilson got into touch first with the Consul and then with the Captain, who were so hospitable, so generous, so kind, that Aunt Martha bought a red rose for her cap, drank champagne, took a hand at cards, and was taught to waltz by Mr. Brown. Their gaieties were cut short, however; a letter demanded Mrs. Wilson's instant presence in London, and Aunt Martha, deposited in Charmouth, could only regret that she had not seen something of life a little sooner, and declare that there "was a boldness and grandeur about the views in Cornwall which far exceeded anything she had seen in Devonshire".

Involved once more with Meylers, Lornes, Lambtons, Berkeleys, Leicesters, gossiping as usual in her box at the Opera about this lady and that gentleman, letting young noblemen pull her hair, tapping late at night at Lord Hertford's little private gate in Park Lane, Harriette's life wound in and out among the bogs and precipices of the shadowy underworld which lies on the far side of the sword. Occasionally the jingling and junketing was interrupted by a military figure; the great Duke himself, very like a ratcatcher in his red ribbon, marched in; asked questions; left money; said he remembered her; had dreamed of her in Spain. "I dreamed you came out on my staff," he said. Or there was Lord Byron sitting entirely alone, dressed in brown flowing robes at a masquerade, "bright, severe, beautiful", demanding "in a tone of wild and thrilling despondency 'Who shall console us for acute bodily anguish?'" Or again the spangled curtain goes up and we see those famous entertainers the sisters Wilson sitting at home at their ease, sparring and squabbling and joking about their lovers; Amy, who adored black puddings; good-natured Fanny, who doted upon donkey-riding; foolish Sophie, who was made a Peeress by Lord Berwick and dropped her sisters; Moll Raffles, Julia, niece to Lord Carysfort and daughter to a maid of honour with the finest legs in Europe—there they sit gossiping profanely and larding their chatter with quotations from Shakespeare and Sterne. Some died prematurely; some married and turned virtuous; some became villains, sorceresses, serpents, and had best be forgotten; while as for Harriette herself, she was scandalously treated by the Beauforts, had to retire to France with her Colonel, would continue to tell the truth about her fine friends so long as they treated her as they did, and grew, we cannot doubt, into a fat good-humoured disreputable old woman who never doubted the goodness of God or denied that the world had treated her well, or regretted, even when the darkness of obscurity and poverty blotted her entirely from view, that she had lived her life on the shady side of the sword.

Genius

"GENIUS," cried Haydon, darting at his canvas after some momentary rebuff, "Genius is sent into the world not to obey laws, but to give them!" But he need not have said it. Genius is written large all over his memoirs. It is genius of a peculiar kind, of course. It is not the Shakespearean but the Victorian genius, not the conscious but the unconscious, not the true, but—let us pause, however, and read Haydon's diaries with attention (they are now reprinted, with a brilliant introduction by Mr. Huxley) before we decide what kind of genius his was. That it was violent in its symptoms and remorseless in its severity, no one can doubt. Of all those men and women who have been stricken with genius (and the number in the British Isles must be great) none suffered more, or was more terribly its victim than the inspired boy with weak eyes who should have been a bookseller in his father's shop in Plymouth, but heard himself summoned to go to London, to be a great painter, to honour his country, and to "rescue the Art from that stigma of incapacity which was impressed on it".

He came to London. He made friends with Wilkie. He lived and painted in one room, and there, night after night, Wilkie, Du Fresne, Dr. Millingen, McClaggan, Allan ("the celebrated painter") and Callender all met and drank his good tea out of his large cups, and argued about art and politics and divinity and medicine and how Marie Antoinette's head was cut off (Du Fresne said he had been present and had flung his red cap into the air), while Liz of Rathbone Place, who loved their talk but was otherwise cold, sided with one, attacked another, and was found studying *Reid on the Human Mind* "with an expression of profound bewilderment". "Happy period!", Haydon burst out, "no servants—no responsibilities—reputation on the bud —ambition beginning, friends untried", and so things might have gone on had it not been for the demon which possessed

Written in 1926

150

him—the devil which made him, even in those early days, indite letters, which Liz applauded, against the might of the Royal Academy, and vow to bring about their humiliation and the triumph of High Art by vast pictures of Dentatus and Macbeth and Solomon, which took months to paint, filled his living-room with the reek of oil, required that he should dissect the forequarters of an ass, bring Guardsmen on their horses into his studio, and run into debt, for, as he soon found out, "the expenses of a work of High Art in England are dreadful".

But there was another consequence of his prepossession. High Art being of necessity large art into the bargain, only the great nobles could afford it, and in consequence the simple life with Liz and cups of good tea was abandoned for the life, or at least the dinner tables, of the Mulgraves and the Beaumonts and any other lord or lady who could be hypnotised into the belief that it was their wish to have a vast picture of Achilles in the drawing-room, and to their credit to have a man of genius talking very loud at their board. Haydon, rapt in his burning enthusiasm for the Heroic and for the Elgin Marbles and for himself, took it all seriously. He entertained fashion all day long. Instead of painting, "I walked about my room, looked into the glass, anticipated what the foreign ambassadors would say," overhead whispers at parties, "he himself has an antique head," and seriously believed, when the beauties put up their eyeglasses and lisped their admiration, that his fortune was made, and that "all the sovereigns of Europe would hail with delight an English youth who could paint an heroic picture". But he was disillusioned. The great, he found, care not for art, but for what people say about pictures. "Dear Lord Mulgrave" lost his faith in Dentatus when he heard it criticised. Sir George Beaumont shillied and shallied and said at last that Macbeth was too big and Lady Beaumont had no room for it, and, "in fact, Sir George was tired and wanted another extra-ordinary young man, for Wilkie was an old story, and I was a nuisance". "And so, artists," he concluded, summing up all that he had borne from his patrons, but letting us infer how boldly he had corrected them and how terribly he had bored them, "and so, artists, be humble and discreet!"

He proved the wisdom of his own saying by marrying, in

spite of his debts, a widow with two children, and by having in quick succession, six more children of his own. With all this weight on his shoulders he sank steadily more and more deeply into the mud. For his genius never deserted him. It was always flourishing irresistible subjects before his eyes. He was always rushing at his canvas and "rubbing in" the head of Alexander "gloriously", or dashing off some gigantic group of warriors and lions when his room was bare of necessities, his furniture pawned, his wife screaming in childbirth, and the baby (it was a a way they had) sickening of a mortal illness. Where a smaller man would have been content to deal with private difficulties, Haydon took upon himself the cares of the world. He was feverishly interested in politics, in the Reform Bill, in the Trades Union movement, in the success of the British arms. Above all, he was the champion of the High Art in England. He must badger Wellington, Peel, and every Minister in turn to employ young English painters to decorate Westminster Hall and the Houses of Parliament. Nor could he let the Royal Academy sleep in peace. His friends begged him to stop; but no. "The idea of being a Luther or a John Knox in art got the better of my reason. . . . I attacked the Academy. I exposed their petty intrigues; I laid open their ungrateful, cruel, and heartless treatment of Wilkie. I annihilated Payne Knight's absurd theories against great works. I proved his ignorance of Pliny", with the result that "I had brought forty men and all their high connections on my back at twenty-six years old, and there was nothing left but Victory or Westminster Abbey. I made up my mind for the conflict, and ordered at once a larger canvas for another work."

But on the road to Victory and Westminster Abbey lay a more sordid lodging-house, through which Haydon passed four times—the King's Bench Prison. Servants and children, he noted, became familiar with the signs of an approaching execution. He himself learned how to pawn and how to plead, how to flatter the sheriff's officer, how to bombard the great, who were certainly generous if they were not clever; how to appeal to the hearts of landlords, whose humanity was extraordinary; but one thing he could not do: deny the demands of his own genius. Portrait painting was an obvious resource.

But then how odious to paint a little private individual, a mere Mayor, or Member of Parliament, when one's head was swarming with Solomons and Jerusalems and Pharaohs and Crucifixions and Macbeths! He could scarcely bring himself to do it. One could make them larger than life, it is true, but then the critics sneered and said that if the ex-Mayor was the size that Haydon painted him, he must have stuck in the doorway. It was paltry work. "The trash that one is obliged to talk! The stuff that one is obliged to copy! The fidgets that are obliged to be borne! My God!"

The name of God was often on his lips. He was on terms of cordial intimacy with the deity. He could not believe that one great spirit could consent to the downfall of another. God and Napoleon and Nelson and Wellington and Haydon were all of the same calibre, all in the grand style. His mind harped on these great names constantly. And as a matter of fact, though poor Mrs. Haydon would smile when he bade her "trust in God", his trust was often justified. He left his house in the morning with the children fighting, with Mary scolding, with no water in the cistern, to trudge all day from patron to pawn-shop, and came home at night "tired, croaking, grumbling and muddy", when, just as hope seemed extinct, a letter arrived; it was from Lord Grey; it contained a cheque. Once more they were saved.

With it all, he declared, he was a very happy man, pink and plump, in spite of all his worries, when Wilkie, who led an abstemious bachelor's life, was cadaverous and plaintive. Now and again they took the children to the sea or snatched an afternoon in Kensington Gardens, and if they were in the depths of despair on Wednesday, likely enough some stroke of fortune would put them in the seventh heaven by Thursday. He had his friends, too—Wordsworth and Scott and Keats and Lamb—with whom he supped and he talked. He had, above all, a mind which was for ever tossing and tumbling like a vigorous dolphin in the seas of thought. "I never feel alone", he wrote, "with visions of ancient heroes, pictures of Christ, principles of ancient Art, humorous subjects, deductions, sarcasms against the Academy, piercing remembrance of my dear children all crowding upon me, I paint, I write, conceive, fall asleep . . . lamenting my mortality at being fatigued." The power which drove him to these extremities did at least reward him with some of its delights.

But as the symptoms of inspiration multiply—this passionate joy in creation, this conviction of a divine mission—one asks oneself what then is false, for falsity there certainly seems to be. First there is something in the superabundance of protest, in the sense of persecution, which rouses suspicion; next these vast pictures of crowds, armies, raptures, agonies begin, even as he sketches them in words, to scar and wound our eyes; and finally we catch ourselves thinking, as some felicity of phrase flashes out or some pose or arrangement makes its effect, that his genius is a writer's. He should have held a pen; of all painters, surely he was the best read. "The truth is I am fonder of books than of anything else on earth", he wrote. He clung to his Shakespeare and his Homer when his lay figure had to go to the pawnbroker. There was even one moment when he doubted his own vocation and accused the sublime art of hampering his powers. But his instinct to express himself in words was undeniable. Overworked as he was, he always found time to write a diary which is in no way perfunctory, but follows with ease and sinuosity the ins and outs of his life. Phrases form naturally at the tip of his pen. "He sat and talked easily, lazily, gazing at the sun with his legs crossed", he says of Chantrey. "Poor fellow," he wrote on hearing of the burial of Wilkie at sea, "I wonder what the fish think of him, with their large glassy eyes in the gurgling deep." Always his painter's eye lights up his phrases, and scenes which would have been repulsive in paint shape themselves naturally and rightly into words. It was some malicious accident that made him, when he had to choose a medium, pick up a brush when the pen lay handy.

But if accident it was, his genius was unrelenting. Paint he must; paint he did. When his cartoons were rejected he learned to toss off pictures of Napoleon Musing, at the rate of one in two hours and a half. When the public deserted his last exhibition in favour of Tom Thumb next door, he darted at another picture, finished the Saxon Lord, dashed in Alfred, "worked", he declared, "gloriously". But at last even his prayers sound a little hoarse, and his protests without conviction. One morning after quoting Lear and writing out a list of his debts and his thoughts, he put a pistol to his forehead, gashed a razor across his throat, and spattered his unfinished picture of Alfred and the first British Jury with his blood. He was the faithful servant of genius to the last. If we seek now any relic of all those acres of canvas, those crowds of heroes, we find clean white walls, people comfortably dining, and a vague rumour that a big picture did hang here once, but the management took it away when the place was done up. The pictures are vanished; Allan, "the celebrated painter", Du Fresne, who saw Marie Antoinette executed, Millingen, Liz of Rathbone Place, all are passed away; but still these pages that he scribbled without thought of Genius or Art or Posterity remain, holding vividly before us the struggling, greedy life with all its black smoke and its flame.

The Enchanted Organ

THE enormous respectability of Bloomsbury was broken one
fine morning about 1840 by the sound of an organ and by
the sight of a little girl who had escaped from her nurse and
was dancing to the music. The child was Thackeray's elder
daughter, Anne. For the rest of her long life, through war and
peace, calamity and prosperity, Miss Thackeray, or Mrs.
Richmond Ritchie, or Lady Ritchie, was always escaping from
the Victorian gloom and dancing to the strains of her own
enchanted organ. The music, at once so queer and so sweet, so
merry and so plaintive, so dignified and so fantastical, is to be
heard very distinctly on every page of the present volume.[1]

For Lady Ritchie was incapable at any stage of her career of
striking an attitude or hiding a feeling. The guns are firing from
Cremorne for the taking of Sebastopol, and there she sits
scribbling brilliant nonsense in her diary about "matches and
fairy tales". "Brother Tomkins at the Oratory is starving and
thrashing himself because he thinks it is right", and Miss
Thackeray is reading novels on Sunday morning "because I
do not think it is wrong". As for religion and her grandmother's
miseries and the clergyman's exhortations to follow "the one
true way", all she knows is that it is her business to love
her father and grandmother, and for the rest she supposes
characteristically "that everybody is right and nobody knows
anything".

Seen through this temperament, at once so buoyant and so
keen, the gloom of that famous age dissolves in an iridescent
mist which lifts entirely to display radiant prospects of glitter-
ing spring, or clings to the monstrous shoulders of its prophets
in many-tinted shreds. There are Mr. FitzGerald and Mr.
Spedding coming to dinner "as kind and queer and melan-

Written in 1924

[1] *Letters of Anne Thackeray Ritchie*, selected and edited by her
daughter, Hester Ritchie.

choly as men could be"; and Mrs. Norton "looking like a beautiful slow sphinx"; and Arthur Prinsep riding in Rotten Row with violets in his buttonhole—" 'I like your violets very much,' said I, and of course they were instantly presented to me"—and Carlyle vociferating that a cheesemite might as well understand a cow as we human mites our maker's secrets; and George Eliot, with her steady little eyes, enunciating a prodigious sentence about building one's cottage in a valley, and the power of influence, and respecting one's work, which breaks off in the middle; and Herbert Spencer stopping a Beethoven sonata with "Thank you, I'm getting flushed"; and Ruskin asserting that "if you can draw a strawberry you can draw anything"; and Mrs. Cameron paddling about in cold water till two in the morning; and Jowett's four young men looking at photographs and sipping tumblers of brandy and water until at last "poor Miss Stephen", who has been transplanted to an island where "everybody is either a genius, or a poet, or a painter, or peculiar in some way", ejaculates in despair, "Is there *nobody* commonplace?"

"Poor Miss Stephen", bored and bewildered, staying with several cousins at the hotel, represented presumably the Puritanical conscience of the nineteenth century when confronted by a group of people who were obviously happy but not obviously bad. On the next page, however, Miss Stephen is significantly "strolling about in the moonlight"; on the next she has deserted her cousins, left the hotel, and is staying with the Thackerays in the centre of infection. The most ingrained Philistine could not remain bored, though bewildered she might be, by Miss Thackeray's charm. For it was a charm extremely difficult to analyse. She said things that no human being could possibly mean; yet she meant them. She lost trains, mixed names, confused numbers, driving up to Town, for example, precisely a week before she was expected, and making Charles Darwin laugh—"I can't for the life of me help laughing," he apologised. But then, if she had gone on the right day, poor Mr. Darwin would have been dying. So with her writing, too. Her novel *Angelica* "went off suddenly to Australia with her feet foremost, and the proofs all wrong and end first!!!" But somehow nobody in Australia found out.

Fortune rewarded the generous trust she put in it. But if her random ways were charming, who, on the other hand, could be more practical, or see things, when she liked, precisely as they were? Old Carlyle was a god on one side of his face but a "cross-grained, ungrateful, self-absorbed old nutcracker" on the other. Her most typical, and, indeed, inimitable sentences rope together a handful of swiftly gathered opposites. To embrace oddities and produce a charming, laughing harmony from incongruities was her genius in life and in letters. "I have just ordered", she writes, "two shillings' worth of poetry for my fisherman . . . we take little walks together, and he carries his shrimps and talks quite enchantingly." She pays the old dropsical woman's fare in the omnibus, and in return the "nice jolly nun hung with crucifixes" escorts her across the road. Nun and fisherman and dropsical old woman had never till that moment, one feels sure, realised their own charm or the gaiety of existence. She was a mistress of phrases which exalt and define and set people in the midst of a comedy. With Nature, too, her gift was equally happy. She would glance out of the window of a Brighton lodging-house and say: "The sky was like a divine parrot's breast, just now, with a deep, deep, flapping sea". As life drew on, with its deaths and its wars, her profound instinct for happiness had to exert itself to gild those grim faces golden, but it succeeded. Even Lord Kitchener and Lord Roberts and the South African War shine transmuted. As for the homelier objects which she preferred, the birds and the downs and the old charwoman "who has been an old angel, without wings, alas! and only a bad leg", and the smut-black chimney-sweeps, who were "probably gods in disguise", they never cease to the very end to glow and twinkle with merriment in her pages. For she was no visionary. Her happiness was a domestic flame, tried by many sorrows. And the music to which she dances, frail and fantastic, but true and distinct, will sound on outside our formidable residences when all the brass bands of literature have (let us hope) blared themselves to perdition.

Two Women

UP to the beginning of the nineteenth century the distinguished woman had almost invariably been an aristocrat. It was the great lady who ruled and wrote letters and influenced the course of politics. From the huge middle class few women rose to eminence, nor has the drabness of their lot received the attention which has been bestowed upon the splendours of the great and the miseries of the poor. There they remain, even in the early part of the nineteenth century, a vast body, living, marrying, bearing children in dull obscurity, until at last we begin to wonder whether there was something in their condition itself—in the age at which they married, the number of children they bore, the privacy they lacked, the incomes they had not, the conventions which stifled them, and the education they never received—which so affected them that, though the middle class is the great reservoir from which we draw our distinguished men, it has thrown up singularly few women to set beside them.

The profound interest of Lady Stephen's life of Miss Emily Davies [1] lies in the light it throws upon this dark and obscure chapter of human history. Miss Davies was born in the year 1830, of middle-class parents who could afford to educate their sons but not their daughters. Her education was, she supposed, much the same as that of other clergymen's daughters at that time. "Do they go to school? No. Do they have governesses at home? No. They have lessons and get on as they can." But if their positive education had stopped at a little Latin, a little history, a little housework, it would not so much have mattered. It was what may be called the negative education, that which decrees not what you may do but what you may not do, that cramped and stifled. "Probably only women who have laboured under it can understand the weight of dis-

Written in 1927
[1] *Emily Davies and Girton College*, by Lady Stephen.

couragement produced by being perpetually told that, as women, nothing much is ever expected of them. . . . Women who have lived in the atmosphere produced by such teaching know how it stifles and chills; how hard it is to work courageously through it." Preachers and rulers of both sexes nevertheless formulated the creed and enforced it vigorously. Charlotte Yonge wrote: "I have no hesitation in declaring my full belief in the inferiority of woman, nor that she brought it upon herself". She reminded her sex of a painful incident with a snake in a garden which had settled their destiny, Miss Yonge said, for ever. The mention of Women's Rights made Queen Victoria so furious that "she cannot contain herself". Mr. Greg, underlining his words, wrote that "the essentials of a woman's being are *that they are supported by, and they minister to, men*". The only other occupation allowed them, indeed, was to become a governess or a needlewoman, "and both these employments were naturally overstocked". If women wanted to paint, there was, up to the year 1858, only one life class in London where they could learn. If they were musical there was the inevitable piano, but the chief aim was to produce a brilliant mechanical execution, and Trollope's picture of four girls all in the same room playing on four pianos, all of them out of tune, seems to have been, as Trollope's pictures usually are, based on fact. Writing was the most accessible of the arts, and write they did, but their books were deeply influenced by the angle from which they were forced to observe the world. Half occupied, always interrupted, with much leisure but little time to themselves and no money of their own, these armies of listless women were either driven to find solace and occupation in religion, or, if that failed, they took, as Miss Nightingale said, "to that perpetual day dreaming which is so dangerous". Some, indeed, envied the working classes, and Miss Martineau frankly hailed the ruin of her family with delight. "I, who had been obliged to write before breakfast, or in some private way, had henceforth liberty to do my own work in my own way, for we had lost our gentility." But the time had come when there were occasional exceptions, both among parents and among daughters. Mr. Leigh Smith, for example, allowed his daughter Barbara the same income that he gave his sons. She at once started a school of an advanced character. Miss Garrett became a doctor because her parents, though shocked and anxious, would be reconciled if she were a success. Miss Davies had a brother who sympathised and helped her in her determination to reform the education of women. With such encouragement the three young women started in the middle of the nineteenth century to lead the army of the unemployed in search of work. But the war of one sex upon the rights and possessions of the other is by no means a straightforward affair of attack and victory or defeat. Neither the means nor the end itself is clear-cut and recognised. There is the very potent weapon, for example, of feminine charm—what use were they to make of that? Miss Garrett said she felt "so mean in trying to come over the doctors by all kinds of little feminine dodges". Mrs. Gurney admitted the difficulty, but pointed out that "Miss Marsh's success among the navvies" had been mainly won by these means, which, for good or bad, were certainly of immense weight. It was agreed therefore that charm was to be employed. Thus we have the curious spectacle, at once so diverting and so humiliating, of grave and busy women doing fancy work and playing croquet in order that the male eye might be gratified and deceived. "Three lovely girls" were placed conspicuously in the front row at a meeting, and Miss Garrett herself sat there looking "exactly like one of the girls whose instinct it is to do what you tell them". For the arguments that they had to meet by these devious means were in themselves extremely indefinite. There was a thing called "the tender home-bloom of maidenliness" which must not be touched. There was chastity, of course, and her handmaidens, innocence, sweetness, unselfishness, sympathy; all of which might suffer if women were allowed to learn Latin and Greek. The *Saturday Review* gave cogent expression to what men feared for women and needed of women in the year 1864. The idea of submitting young ladies to local university examinations "almost takes one's breath away", the writer said. If examined they must be, steps must be taken to see that "learned men advanced in years" were the examiners, and that the presumably aged wives of these aged gentlemen should occupy "a commanding position in the gallery". Even so it would be "next to impossible to persuade the world that a pretty first-class woman came by her honours fairly". For the truth was, the reviewer wrote, that "there is a strong and ineradicable male instinct that a learned or even an accomplished young woman is the most intolerable monster in creation". It was against instincts and prejudices such as these, tough as roots but intangible as sea mist, that Miss Davies had to fight. Her days passed in a round of the most diverse occupations. Besides the actual labour of raising money and fighting prejudice, she had to decide the most delicate moral questions which, directly victory was within sight, began to be posed by the students and their parents. A mother, for example, would only entrust her with her daughter's education on condition that she should come home "as if nothing had happened," and not "take to anything eccentric". The students, on the other hand, bored with watching the Edinburgh express slip a carriage at Hitchin or rolling the lawn with a heavy iron roller, took to playing football, and then invited their teachers to see them act scenes from Shakespeare and Swinburne dressed in men's clothes. This indeed was a very serious matter; the great George Eliot was consulted; Mr. Russell Gurney was consulted, and also Mr. Tomkinson. They decided that it was unwomanly; Hamlet must be played in a skirt.

Miss Davies herself was decidedly austere. When money for the college flowed in she refused to spend it on luxuries. She wanted rooms—always more and more rooms to house those unhappy girls dreaming their youth away in indolence or picking up a little knowledge in the family sitting-room. "Privacy was the one luxury Miss Davies desired for the student, and in her eyes it was not a luxury—she despised luxuries—but a necessity." But one room to themselves was enough. She did not believe that they needed armchairs to sit in or pictures to look at. She herself lived austerely in lodgings till she was seventy-two, combative, argumentative, frankly preferring a labour meeting at Venice to the pictures and the palaces, consumed with an abstract passion for justice to women which burnt up trivial personalities and made her a little intolerant of social frivolities. Was it worth while, she once asked, in her admirable, caustic manner, after meeting Lady Augusta Stanley, to go among the aristocracy? "I felt directly that if I went to Lady Stanley's again I must get a new bonnet. And is it well to spend one's money in bonnets and flys instead of on instructive books?" she wondered. For Miss Davies perhaps was a little deficient in feminine charm.

That was a charge that nobody could bring against Lady Augusta Stanley. No two women could on the surface have less in common. Lady Augusta, it is true, was no more highly educated in a bookish sense than the middle-class women whom Miss Davies championed. But she was the finest flower of the education which for some centuries the little class of aristocratic women had enjoyed. She had been trained in her mother's drawing-room in Paris. She had talked to all the distinguished men and women of her time—Lamartine, Merimée, Victor Hugo, the Duc de Broglie, Sainte-Beuve, Renan, Jenny Lind, Turgenev—everybody came to talk to old Lady Elgin and to be entertained by her daughters. There she developed that abounding sensibility, that unquenchable sympathy which were to be so lavishly drawn upon in after years. For she was very young when she entered the Duchess of Kent's household. For fifteen years of her youth she lived there. For fifteen years she was the life and soul of that "quiet affectionate dull household of old people at Frogmore and Clarence House". Nothing whatever happened. They drove out and she thought how charming the village children looked. They walked and the Duchess picked heather. They came home and the Duchess was tired. Yet not for a moment, pouring her heart out in profuse letters to her sisters, does she complain or wish for any other existence.

Seen through her peculiar magnifying-glass the slightest event in the life of the Royal Family was either harrowing in the extreme or beyond words delightful. Prince Arthur was more handsome than ever. The Princess Helena was so lovely. Princess Ada fell from her pony. Prince Leo was naughty. The Beloved Duchess wanted a green umbrella. The measles had come out, but, alas, they threatened to go in again. One might suppose, to listen to Lady Augusta exclaiming and protesting in alternate rapture and despair, that to read aloud to the old Duchess of Kent was the most exciting of occupations, and that the old lady's rheumatisms and headaches were catastrophes of the first order. For inevitably the power of sympathy, when so highly developed and discharged solely upon personal relations, tends to produce a hothouse atmosphere in which domestic details assume prodigious proportions and the mind feeds upon every detail of death and disease with a gluttonous relish. The space devoted in this volume[1] to illness and marriage entirely outweighs any reference to art, literature, or politics. It is all personal, emotional, and detailed as one of the novels which were written so inevitably by women.

It was such a life as this, and such an atmosphere as this, that Mr. Greg and the *Saturday Review* and many men, who had themselves enjoyed the utmost rigours of education, wished to see preserved. And perhaps there was some excuse for them. It is difficult to be sure, after all, that a college don is the highest type of humanity known to us; and there is something in Lady Augusta's power to magnify the common and illumine the dull which seems to imply a very arduous education of some sort behind it. Nevertheless as one studies the lives of the two women side by side one cannot doubt that Miss Davies got more interest, more pleasure, and more use out of one month of her life than Lady Augusta out of a whole year of hers. Some inkling of the fact seems to have reached Lady Augusta even at Windsor Castle. Perhaps being a woman of the old type is a little exhausting; perhaps it is not altogether satisfying. Lady Augusta at any rate seems to have got wind of other possibilities. She liked the society of literary people best, she said. "I had always said that I had wished to be a fellow of a college," she added surprisingly. At any rate she was one of the first to support Miss Davies in her demand for a University education for women. Did Miss Davies sacrifice her book and buy her bonnet? Did the two women, so different in every other way, come together over this—the education of their sex? It is tempting to think so, and to imagine sprung from that union of the middle-class woman and the court lady some astonishing phoenix of the future who shall combine the new efficiency with the old amenity, the courage of the indomitable Miss Davies and Lady Augusta's charm.

[1] *Letters of Lady Augusta Stanley*, edited by the Dean of Windsor and Hector Bolitho.

Ellen Terry

WHEN she came on to the stage as Lady Cicely in *Captain Brassbound's Conversion*, the stage collapsed like a house of cards and all the limelights were extinguished. When she spoke it was as if someone drew a bow over a ripe, richly seasoned 'cello; it grated, it glowed, and it growled. Then she stopped speaking. She put on her glasses. She gazed intently at the back of a settee. She had forgotten her part. But did it matter? Speaking or silent, she was Lady Cicely—or was it Ellen Terry? At any rate, she filled the stage and all the other actors were put out, as electric lights are put out in the sun.

Yet this pause when she forgot what Lady Cicely said next was significant. It was a sign not that she was losing her memory and past her prime, as some said. It was a sign that Lady Cicely was not a part that suited her. Her son, Gordon Craig, insists that she only forgot her part when there was something uncongenial in the words, when some speck of grit had got into the marvellous machine of her genius. When the part was congenial, when she was Shakespeare's Portia, Desdemona, Ophelia, every word, every comma was consumed. Even her eyelashes acted. Her body lost its weight. Her son, a mere boy, could lift her in his arms. "I am not myself," she said. "Something comes upon me. . . . I am always-in-the-air, light and bodiless." We, who can only remember her as Lady Cicely on the little stage at the Court Theatre, only remember what, compared with her Ophelia or her Portia, was as a picture postcard compared with the great Velasquez in the gallery.

It is the fate of actors to leave only picture postcards behind them. Every night when the curtain goes down the beautiful coloured canvas is rubbed out. What remains is at best only a wavering, insubstantial phantom—a verbal life on the lips of the living. Ellen Terry was well aware of it. She tried herself,

Written in January 1941

overcome by the greatness of Irving as Hamlet and indignant
at the caricatures of his detractors, to describe what she remembered. It was in vain. She dropped her pen in despair.
"Oh God, that I were a writer!" she cried. "Surely a *writer*
could not string words together about Henry Irving's Hamlet
and say *nothing*, *nothing*." It never struck her, humble as she
was, and obsessed by her lack of book learning, that she was,
among other things, a writer. It never occurred to her when
she wrote her autobiography, or scribbled page after page to
Bernard Shaw late at night, dead tired after a rehearsal, that
she was "writing". The words in her beautiful rapid hand
bubbled off her pen. With dashes and notes of exclamation she
tried to give them the very tone and stress of the spoken word.
It is true, she could not build a house with words, one room
opening out of another, and a staircase connecting the whole.
But whatever she took up became in her warm, sensitive grasp
a tool. If it was a rolling-pin, she made perfect pastry. If it was
a carving knife, perfect slices fell from the leg of mutton. If it
were a pen, words peeled off, some broken, some suspended in
mid-air, but all far more expressive than the tappings of the
professional typewriter.

With her pen then at odds and ends of time she has painted
a self-portrait. It is not an Academy portrait, glazed, framed,
complete. It is rather a bundle of loose leaves upon each of
which she has dashed off a sketch for a portrait—here a nose,
here an arm, here a foot, and there a mere scribble in the
margin. The sketches done in different moods, from different
angles, sometimes contradict each other. The nose cannot
belong to the eyes; the arm is out of all proportion to the foot.
It is difficult to assemble them. And there are blank pages, too.
Some very important features are left out. There was a self she
did not know, a gap she could not fill. Did she not take Walt
Whitman's words for a motto? "Why, even I myself, I often
think, know little or nothing of my real life. Only a few hints—
a few diffused faint clues and indirections. . . . I seek . . . to
trace out here."

Nevertheless, the first sketch is definite enough. It is the
sketch of her childhood. She was born to the stage. The stage
was her cradle, her nursery. When other little girls were being

taught sums and pot-hooks she was being cuffed and buffeted into the practice of her profession. Her ears were boxed, her muscles suppled. All day she was hard at work on the boards. Late at night when other children were safe in bed she was stumbling along the dark streets wrapped in her father's cloak. And the dark street with its curtained windows was nothing but a sham to that little professional actress, and the rough and tumble life on the boards was her home, her reality. "It's all such sham there", she wrote—meaning by "there" what she called "life lived in houses"—"sham—cold—hard— pretending. It's not sham here in our theatre—here all is real, warm and kind—we live a lovely spiritual life here."

That is the first sketch. But turn to the next page. The child born to the stage has become a wife. She is married at sixteen to an elderly famous painter. The theatre has gone; its lights are out and in its place is a quiet studio in a garden. In its place is a world full of pictures and "gentle artistic people with quiet voices and elegant manners". She sits mum in her corner while the famous elderly people talk over her head in quiet voices. She is content to wash her husband's brushes; to sit to him; to play her simple tunes on the piano to him while he paints. In the evening she wanders over the Downs with the great poet, Tennyson. "I was in Heaven," she wrote. "I never had one single pang of regret for the theatre." If only it could have lasted! But somehow—here a blank page intervenes—she was an incongruous element in that quiet studio. She was too young, too vigorous, too vital, perhaps. At any rate, the marriage was a failure.

And so, skipping a page or two, we come to the next sketch. She is a mother now. Two adorable children claim all her devotion. She is living in the depths of the country, in the heart of domesticity. She is up at six. She scrubs, she cooks, she sews. She teaches the children. She harnesses the pony. She fetches the milk. And again she is perfectly happy. To live with children in a cottage, driving her little cart about the lanes, going to church on Sunday in blue and white cotton—that is the ideal life! She asks no more than that it shall go on like that for ever and ever. But one day the wheel comes off the pony cart. Huntsmen in pink leap over the hedge. One of them dismounts and offers help. He looks at the girl in a blue frock and exclaims; "Good God! It's Nelly!" She looks at the huntsman in pink and cries, "Charles Reade!" And so, all in a jiffy, back she goes to the stage, and to forty pounds a week. For—that is the reason she gives—the bailiffs are in the house. She must make money.

At this point a very blank page confronts us. There is a gulf which we can only cross at a venture. Two sketches face each other; Ellen Terry in blue cotton among the hens; Ellen Terry robed and crowned as Lady Macbeth on the stage of the Lyceum. The two sketches are contradictory yet they are both of the same woman. She hates the stage; yet she adores it. She worships her children; yet she forsakes them. She would like to live for ever among pigs and ducks in the open air; yet she spends the rest of her life among actors and actresses in the limelight. Her own attempt to explain the discrepancy is hardly convincing. "I have always been more woman than artist," she says. Irving put the theatre first. "He had none of what I may call my bourgeois qualities—the love of being in love, the love of a home, the dislike of solitude." She tries to persuade us that she was an ordinary woman enough; a better hand at pastry than most; an adept at keeping house; with an eye for colour, a taste for furniture, and a positive passion for washing children's heads. If she went back to the stage it was because—well, what else could she do when the bailiffs were in the house?

This is the little sketch that she offers us to fill in the gap between the two Ellen Terrys—Ellen the mother, and Ellen the actress. But here we remember her warning: "Why, even I myself know little or nothing of my real life." There was something in her that she did not understand; something that came surging up from the depths and swept her away in its clutches. The voice she heard in the lane was not the voice of Charles Reade; nor was it the voice of the bailiffs. It was the voice of her genius; the urgent call of something that she could not define, could not suppress, and must obey. So she left her children and followed the voice back to the stage, back to the Lyceum, back to a long life of incessant toil, anguish, and glory.

But, having gazed at the full-length portrait of Ellen Terry as Sargeant painted her, robed and crowned as Lady Macbeth, turn to the next page. It is done from another angle. Pen in hand, she is seated at her desk. A volume of Shakespeare lies before her. It is open at *Cymbeline*, and she is making careful notes in the margin. The part of Imogen presents great problems. She is, she says, "on the rack" about her interpretation. Perhaps Bernard Shaw can throw light upon the question? A letter from the brilliant young critic of the *Saturday Review* lies beside Shakespeare. She has never met him, but for years they have written to each other, intimately, ardently, disputatiously, some of the best letters in the language. He says the most outrageous things. He compares dear Henry to an ogre, and Ellen to a captive chained in his cage. But Ellen Terry is quite capable of holding her own against Bernard Shaw. She scolds him, laughs at him, fondles him, and contradicts him. She has a curious sympathy for the advanced views that Henry Irving abominated. But what suggestions has the brilliant critic to make about Imogen? None apparently that she has not already thought for herself. She is as close and critical a student of Shakespeare as he is. She has studied every line, weighed the meaning of every word; experimented with every gesture. Each of those golden moments when she becomes bodyless, not herself, is the result of months of minute and careful study. "Art", she quotes, "needs that which we can give her, I assure you." In fact this mutable woman, all instinct, sympathy, and sensation, is as painstaking a student and as careful of the dignity of her art as Flaubert himself.

But once more the expression on that serious face changes. She works like a slave—none harder. But she is quick to tell Mr. Shaw that she does not work with her brain only. She is not in the least clever. Indeed, she is happy she tells him, *"not to be clever"*. She stresses the point with a jab of her pen. "You clever people", as she calls him and his friends, miss so much, mar so much. As for education, she never had a day's schooling in her life. As far as she can see, but the problem baffles her, the main spring of her art is imagination. Visit mad-houses, if you like; take notes; observe; study endlessly. But first, imagine. And so she takes her part away from the books out into the woods.

Rambling down grassy rides, she lives her part until she is it. If a word jars or grates, she must re-think it, re-write it. Then when every phrase is her own, and every gesture spontaneous, out she comes on to the stage and is Imogen, Ophelia, Desdemona.

But is she, even when the great moments are on her, a great actress? She doubts it. "I cared more for love and life," she says. Her face, too, has been no help to her. She cannot sustain emotion. Certainly she is not a great tragic actress. Now and again, perhaps, she has acted some comic part to perfection. But even while she analyses herself, as one artist to another, the sun slants upon an old kitchen chair. "Thank the Lord for my eyes!" she exclaims. What a world of joy her eyes have brought her! Gazing at the old "rush-bottomed, sturdy-legged, and wavy-backed" chair, the stage is gone, the limelights are out, the famous actress is forgotten.

Which, then, of all these women is the real Ellen Terry? How are we to put the scattered sketches together? Is she mother, wife, cook, critic, actress, or should she have been, after all, a painter? Each part seems the right part until she throws it aside and plays another. Something of Ellen Terry it seems overflowed every part and remained unacted. Shakespeare could not fit her; not Ibsen; nor Shaw. The stage could not hold her; nor the nursery. But there is, after all, a greater dramatist than Shakespeare, Ibsen, or Shaw. There is Nature. Hers is so vast a stage, and so innumerable a company of actors, that for the most part she fobs them off with a tag or two. They come on and they go off without breaking the ranks. But now and again Nature creates a new part, an original part. The actors who act that part always defy our attempts to name them. They will not act the stock parts—they forget the words, they improvise others of their own. But when they come on the stage falls like a pack of cards and the limelights are extinguished. That was Ellen Terry's fate—to act a new part. And thus while other actors are remembered because they were Hamlet, Phèdre, or Cleopatra, Ellen Terry is remembered because she was Ellen Terry.

To Spain

You, who cross the Channel yearly, probably no longer see the house at Dieppe, no longer feel, as the train moves slowly down the street, one civilisation fall, another rise—from the ruin and chaos of British stucco this incredible pink and blue phoenix four stories high, with its flower-pots, its balconies, its servant-girl leaning on the window-sill indolently looking out. Quite unmoved you sit reading—Thomas Hardy perhaps —bridging abysses, preserving continuity, a little contemptuous of the excitement which is moving those who feel themselves liberated from one civilisation, launched upon another, to such odd gestures, such strange irreticences. But reflect how much they have already gone through. Try to recall the look of London streets seen very early, perhaps very young, from a cab window on the way to Victoria. Everywhere there is the same intensity, as if the moment instead of moving lay suddenly still, because suddenly solemn, fixed the passers-by in their most transient aspects eternally. They do not know how important they have become. If they did, perhaps they would cease to buy newspapers and scrub doorsteps. But we who are about to leave them feel all the more moved that they should continue to do these homely things on the brink of that precipice—our departure. Therefore it is natural that those who have survived the crossing, with its last scrutiny of passing faces so like a little rehearsal of death, should be shaken; should move handbags; start conversations; and tremble for one intoxicating moment upon the brink of that ideal society where everyone without fear or hesitation reveals the depths of his soul.

But it is only for a moment. Next, the disembodied spirit fluttering at the window desires above all things to be admitted to the new society where the houses are painted in lozenges of pale pink and blue; women wear shawls; trousers are baggy;

Written in 1923

there are crucifixes on hill-tops; yellow mongrel dogs; chairs in the street; cobbles—gaiety, frivolity, drama, in short. "I'm awfully sorry for Agnes because now they can't be married till he gets a job in London. It's too far to get back from the works for midday dinner. I should have thought the father would have done something for them." These detached sentences, spoken a little brokenly (for they are frowning into tiny mirrors and drawing combs intently through fair bobbed hair) by two English girls, fall like the bars of a prison-house heavily across the mind. It is from them that we must escape; the hours, the works, the divisions, rigid and straight, of the old British week. Already as the train moves out of Dieppe these obstructions seem bubbling and boiling in the cauldron of a more congenial civilization. The days of the week diminished; the hours disappeared. It was five o'clock, but no banks had simultaneously shut their doors, nor from innumerable lifts had millions of citizens emerged in time for dinner, or in the poorer suburbs for slices of cold meat and Swiss roll laid orderly in shallow glass dishes. There must be divisions even for the French, but where they fall we cannot tell, and the lady in the corner, so pale, so plump, so compact, seemed as she sat smiling to be riding life over ditches and boundaries smoothed out by the genius of the Latin race.

She rose to go to the dining-car. As she sat down she took a small frying-pan from her handbag and hid it discreetly beneath a tent made from a copy of *Le Temps*. Deftly as each dish was served she secreted a portion in the absence of the waiter. Her husband smiled. Her husband approved. We only knew that she was brave. They might be poor. The helpings were large. The French have mothers. To redress perpetually the extravagances of life, and make the covering fit the fact instead of bulging in ostentatious emptiness, was part, no doubt, of the French genius for living. Still, when it comes to the thick yellow rind of a not fresh cheese—. Ironically smiling, she condescended, in that exquisite tongue which twinkles like diamonds with all its accents, to explain that she kept a dog. But she might have kept—anything. "Life is so simple," she seemed to say.

"Life is so simple—life is so simple," said the wheels of the

Sud Express all night long, in that idiotic or ironic way they have, for any message less appropriate to the uneasy darkness, the clank of chains, the anguished cries of railwaymen, and in the dawn the misery of the unrested body, could scarcely be imagined. But travellers are much at the mercy of phrases. Taken from home, which like a shell has made them hard, separate, individual, vast generalisations formulate in their exposed brains; the stress of wheel or window-blind beats into rhythm idiotic sayings of false profundity about life, repeats to distraction fragments of prose, and makes them stare with ferocious melancholy at the landscape, which in the middle of France is dull enough. The French are methodical; but life is simple; the French are prosaic; the French have roads. Yes, they have roads which strike from that lean poplar there to Vienna, to Moscow; pass Tolstoy's house, climb mountains, then march, all shop decorated, down the middle of famous cities. But in England the road runs out on to a cliff; wavers into sand at the edge of the sea. It begins to seem dangerous to live in England. Here actually one could build a house and have no neighbours; go for a walk along this eternal white road for two, three, four miles, and meet only one black dog and one old woman who, depressed perhaps by the immensity of the landscape and the futility of locomotion, has sat herself down on a bank, attached her cow to her by a rope, and there sits, unmoved, incurious, monumental. Could our English poets for a moment share her seat and think her thoughts, forget the parish, the pansy, and the sparrow's egg, and concentrate (as she appears to do) upon the fate of men!

But as the country grows larger and larger outside Bordeaux, the concentration which is needed to produce even the simplest of little thoughts is rent as a glove is torn by the thrust of a large hand. Blessed are painters with their brushes, paints, and canvases. But words are flimsy things. They turn tail at the first approach of visual beauty. They let one down in the most literal sense into a chaotic, an alarming chasm filled—for the eye pours it all in—with white towns, with mules in single file, with solitary farms, with enormous churches, with vast fields crumbling at evening into pallor, with fruit-trees blazing askew like blown matches, and trees burning with oranges, and clouds and storms. Beauty seemed to have closed overhead and one washes this way and that in her waters. It is always on the shoulders of a human being that one climbs out; a profile in the corridor; a lady in deep mourning who steps into a motor-car and drives across an arid plain—where and why? a child in Madrid throwing confetti effusively upon the figure of Christ; an Englishman discussing, while his hat obscures half the Sierra Nevada, Mr. Churchill's last article in *The Times*. "No," one says to beauty—as one rebukes an importunate dog, "down, down; let me look at you through the eyes of human beings."

But the Englishman's hat is no measure of the Sierra Nevada. Setting out next day upon foot and mule-back, this wrinkled red and white screen, this background for hats, this queer comment (especially at sunset) upon Mr. Churchill's article in *The Times* is found to consist of stones, olive trees, goats, asphodels, irises, bushes, ridges, shelves, clumps, tufts, and hollows innumerable, indescribable, unthinkable. The mind's contents break into short sentences. It is hot; the old man; the frying-pan; it is hot; the image of the Virgin; the bottle of wine; it is time for lunch; it is only half-past twelve; it is hot. And then over and over again come all those objects—stones, olives, goats, asphodels, dragon-flies, irises, until by some trick of the imagination they run into phrases of command, exhortation, and encouragement such as befit soldiers marching, sentinels on lonely nights, and leaders of great battalions. But must one give up the struggle? Must one relinquish the game? Yes, for the clouds are drifting across the pass; mules mind not what they carry; mules never stumble; they know the way. Why not leave everything to them?

Riders, as night comes on (and the pass was very misty), seem to be riding out of life towards some very enticing prospect, while the four legs of their beasts carry on all necessary transactions with the earth. Riders are at rest; on they go, and on and on. And, they muse, what does it all matter; and what harm can come to a good man (behold two priests stepping out of the drizzle, bowing and disappearing) in life or after death? And then, since a fox has crossed the path, which is on turf and must be nearly at the top of the mountain, how strangely it seems as if they were riding in England, a long day's journey, hundreds of years ago, and the danger is over, and they see the lights of the inn, and the hostess comes into the courtyard and bids them sit round the fire while she cooks dinner, which they do, half-dreaming, while clumsy boys and girls with red flowers pass and repass in the background, and the mother suckles her baby, and the old man who never speaks breaks tufts from the brushwood and throws them on the fire, which blazes up, and the whole company stares.

But good heavens! One never knows what days follow what nights. Good heavens again! "Don Fernando had a passion for pigeon pie, and so kept pigeons up here"—on his roof, that is, from which one has this astonishing, this strange, this disturbing view of the Alpujarras. "He died last summer in Granada." Did he, indeed? It is the light, of course; a million razor-blades have shaved off the bark and the dust, and out pours pure colour; whiteness from fig-trees; red and green and again white from the enormous, the humped, the everlasting landscape. But listen to the sounds on the roof—first the fluttering pigeons; then water rushing; then an old man crying chickens for sale; then a donkey braying in the valley far below. Listen; and as one listens this random life begins to be issued from the heart of a village which has faced the African coast with a timeless and aristocratic endurance for a thousand years. But how say this (as one descends from the blaze) to the Spanish peasant woman who bids one enter her room, with its lilies and its washing, and smiles and looks out of the window as if she too had looked for a thousand years?

Fishing

WHILE there is a Chinese proverb which says that the fisherman is pure at heart "as a white sea-shell", there is a Japanese poem, four lines long, which says something so true but at the same time so crude about the hearts of politicians that it had better be left in its original obscurity. It may be this contradiction—Major Hills, says his publisher, "has been a member of the House of Commons for thirty years. . . . Throughout his long parliamentary life he has remained faithful to his favourite sport"—which has produced a collision in his book; a confusion in the mind of the reader between fish and men.

All books are made of words, but mostly of words that flutter and agitate thought. This book on the contrary, though made of words, has a strange effect on the body. It lifts it out of the chair; stands it on the banks of a river, and strikes it dumb. The river rushes by; a voice commands: "Stand absolutely motionless. . . . Cast up and slightly across. . . . Shoot the line out. . . . Let the flies come well round. . . . On no account pull. . . . Do not be in a hurry to lift. . . ." But the strain is too great, the excitement too intense. We have pulled —we have lifted. The fish is off. "Wait longer next time," the voice commands; "wait longer and longer."

Now, if the art of writing consists in laying an egg in the reader's mind from which springs the thing itself—whether man or fish—and if this art requires such ardour in its practitioners that they will readily, like Flaubert, give up all their bright spring mornings to its pursuit, how does it come about that Major Hills, who has spent thirty years in the House of Commons, can do the trick? Sometimes at four in the morning, in the early spring dawn, he has roused himself, not to dandle words, but to rush down to the river—"the exquisite river, with its vivid green wooded banks, its dark rose-coloured sandstone rocks, its rushing crystalline water", and there he has stood with his rod. There we stand too.

Look at the rod. It was bought of Strong of Carlisle and cost one pound. "It consisted of a piece of whole bamboo with a lancewood top spliced on. . . . Never have I had a rod sweeter to cast with and throwing a longer line." It is not a rod; it is a tool, more beautiful than a Persian pot, more desirable than a lover. ". . . A friend broke it . . . and I could never get another like it . . . and I grieved sorely, for bamboo cannot be mended." What death or disaster could be more pungent? But this is no time for sentiment. There deep under the bank lies the old male salmon. What fly will he take? The grey turkey, with a body of violet silk, the archdeacon in fact, number one? The line is cast; out it floats; down its settles. And then? ". . . The fish went perfectly mad, overran my reel . . . jammed it, and broke my twisted gut trace. It all happened in a few seconds. . . ." But they were seconds of extraordinary intensity, seconds lived alone "in a world of strong emotion, cut off from all else". When we look up Corby's walks have changed. "The trees had their young light leaves, some of them golden, the wild cherry was covered with drifts of snow and the ground was covered with dog mercury, looking as though it had been newly varnished. . . . I felt receptive to every sight, every colour and every sound, as though I walked through a world from which a veil had been withdrawn."

Is it possible that to remove veils from trees it is necessary to fish?—our conscious mind must be all body, and then the unconscious mind leaps to the top and strips off veils? Is it possible that, if to bare reality is to be a poet, we have, as Mr. Yeats said the other day, no great poet because since the war farmers preserve or net their waters, and vermin get up? Has the deplorable habit of Clubs to fetter anglers with ridiculous restrictions, to pamper them with insidious luxuries, somehow cramped our poets' style? And the novelists—if we have no novelist in England to-day whose stature is higher than the third button on Sir Walter's waistcoat, or reaches to the watch-chain of Charles Dickens, or the ring on the little finger of George Eliot, is it not that the Cumberland poachers are dying out? "They were an amusing race, full of rare humour,

delightful to talk to. . . . We often had chats on the banks
and they would tell me quite openly of their successes." But now
"the old wild days are over"; the poachers are gone. They catch
trout, commercially, innumerably, for hotels. Banish from
fiction all poachers' talk, the dialect, the dialogue of Scott, the
publicans, the farmers of Dickens and George Eliot, and what
remains? Mouldy velvet; moth-eaten ermine; mahogany tables;
and a few stuffed fowls. No wonder, since the poachers are
gone, that fiction is failing. . . . "But this is not catching
trout," the voice commands. "Do not dawdle. . . . Start
fishing again without delay."

It is a bad day; the sun is up; the trout are not feeding. We
fail again and again. But fishing teaches a stern morality; in-
culcates a remorseless honesty. The fault may be with ourselves. "Why do I go on missing at the strike? . . . If I had
more delicacy in casting, more accuracy, if I had fished finer,
should I not have done better? And the answer is—Yes! . . .
I lost him through sinning against the light. . . . I failed
through obstinate stupidity." We are sunk deep in the world of
meditation and remorse. "Contradiction lies at the root of all
powerful emotions. We are not ruled by reason. We follow a
different law, and recognise its sanctions. . . ." Sounds from
the outer world come through the roar of the river. Barbarians
have invaded the upper waters of the Eden and Driffield Beck.
But happily the barbarians are grayling; and the profound
difference that divides the human race is a question of bait—
whether to fish with worms or not; some will; to others the
thought is unutterably repulsive.

But the summer's day is fading. Night is coming on—the
Northern night, which is not dark, for the light is there, but
veiled. "A Cumberland night is something to remember",
and trout—for trout are "curious pieces of work"—will feed
in Cumberland at midnight. Let us go down to the bank again.
The river sounds louder than by day. "As I walked down I
heard its varied cadence, obscured during sunlight, at one
moment deep, then clamorous, then where thick beech trees
hid the river subdued to a murmur. . . . The flowering trees
had long since lost their blossoms, but on coming to a syringa
bush I walked suddenly into its scent, and was drenched as in

a bath. I sat on the path. I stretched my legs. I lay down, finding a tuft of grass for pillow, and the yielding sand for mattress. I fell asleep."

And while the fisherman sleeps, we who are presumably reading—but what kind of reading is this when we see through the words Corby's trees and trout at the bottom of the page?—wonder, what does the fisherman dream? Of all the rivers rushing past—the Eden, the Test, and the Kennet, each river different from the other, each full of shadowy fish, and each fish different from the other; the trout subtle, the salmon ingenious; each with its nerves, with its brain, its mentality that we can dimly penetrate, movements we can mystically anticipate, for just as, suddenly, Greek and Latin sort themselves in a flash, so we understand the minds of fish? Or does he dream of the wild Scottish hill in the blizzard; and the patch of windless weather behind the rock, when the pale grasses no longer bent but stood upright; or of the vision on top—twenty Whooper swans floating on the loch fearlessly, "for they had come from some land where they had never seen a man"? Or does he dream of poachers with their whisky-stained weather-beaten faces; or of Andrew Lang, drinking, and discussing the first book of Genesis ; or of F. S. Oliver, whose buttons after a meal "kept popping off like broom pods in autumn"; or of Sparrow, the hunter, "a more generous animal never was seen"; or of the great Arthur Wood and all his bees? Or does he dream of places that his ghost will revisit if it ever comes to earth again—of Ramsbury, Highhead, and the Isle of Jura?

For dream he does. "I always, even now, dream that I shall astonish the world. An outstanding success. . . ." The Premiership is it? No, this triumph, this outstanding success is not with men; it is with fish; it is with the floating line. "I believe it will come. . . ." But here he wakes "with that sense of well-being which sleep in the open air always engenders. It was midnight, moonless and clear. I walked to the edge of the flat rock. . . ." The trout were feeding.

The Artist and Politics

I HAVE been asked by the Artist's International Association to explain as shortly as I can why it is that the artist at present is interested, actively and genuinely, in politics. For it seems that there are some people to whom this interest is suspect.

That the writer is interested in politics needs no saying. Every publisher's list, almost every book that is now issued, brings proof of the fact. The historian to-day is writing not about Greece and Rome in the past, but about Germany and Spain in the present; the biographer is writing lives of Hitler and Mussolini, not of Henry the Eighth and Charles Lamb; the poet introduces communism and fascism into his lyrics; the novelist turns from the private lives of his characters to their social surroundings and their political opinions. Obviously the writer is in such close touch with human life that any agitation in his subject matter must change his angle of vision. Either he focuses his sight upon the immediate problem; or he brings his subject matter into relation with the present; or in some cases, so paralysed is he by the agitations of the moment that he remains silent.

But why should this agitation affect the painter and the sculptor? it may be asked. He is not concerned with the feelings of his model but with its form. The rose and the apple have no political views. Why should he not spend his time contemplating them, as he has always done, in the cold north light that still falls through his studio window?

To answer this question shortly is not easy, for to understand why the artist—the plastic artist—is affected by the state of society, we must try to define the relations of the artist to society, and this is difficult, partly because no such definition has ever been made. But that there is some sort of understanding between them, most people would agree; and in times of peace it may be said roughly to run as follows. The artist on his side held that since the value of his work depended upon freedom of mind, security of person, and immunity from practical affairs—for to mix art with politics, he held, was to adulterate it—he was absolved from political duties; sacrificed many of the privileges that the active citizen enjoyed; and in return created what is called a work of art. Society on its side bound itself to run the state in such a manner that it paid the artist a living wage; asked no active help from him; and considered itself repaid by those works of art which have always formed one of its chief claims to distinction. With many lapses and breaches on both sides, the contract has been kept; society has accepted the artist's work in lieu of other services, and the artist, living for the most part precariously on a pittance, has written or painted without regard for the political agitations of the moment. Thus it would be impossible, when we read Keats, or look at the pictures of Titian and Velasquez, or listen to the music of Mozart or Bach, to say what was the political condition of the age or the country in which these works were created. And if it were otherwise—if the *Ode to a Nightingale* were inspired by hatred of Germany; if *Bacchus and Ariadne* symbolised the conquest of Abyssinia; if *Figaro* expounded the doctrines of Hitler, we should feel cheated and imposed upon, as if, instead of bread made with flour, we were given bread made with plaster.

But if it is true that some such contract existed between the artist and society, in times of peace, it by no means follows that the artist is independent of society. Materially of course he depends upon it for his bread and butter. Art is the first luxury to be discarded in times of stress; the artist is the first of the workers to suffer. But intellectually also he depends upon society. Society is not only his paymaster but his patron. If the patron becomes too busy or too distracted to exercise his critical faculty, the artist will work in a vacuum and his art will suffer and perhaps perish from lack of understanding. Again, if the patron is neither poor nor indifferent, but dictatorial— if he will only buy pictures that flatter his vanity or serve his politics—then again the artist is impeded and his work becomes worthless. And even if there are some artists who can afford to disregard the patron, either because they have private means or have learnt in the course of time to form their own style and to depend upon tradition, these are for the most part only the older artists whose work is already done. Even they, however, are by no means immune. For though it would be easy to stress the point absurdly, still it is a fact that the practice of art, far from making the artist out of touch with his kind, rather increases his sensibility. It breeds in him a feeling for the passions and needs of mankind in the mass which the citizen whose duty it is to work for a particular country or for a particular party has no time and perhaps no need to cultivate. Thus even if he be ineffective, he is by no means apathetic. Perhaps indeed he suffers more than the active citizen because he has no obvious duty to discharge.

For such reasons then it is clear that the artist is affected as powerfully as other citizens when society is in chaos, although the disturbance affects him in different ways. His studio now is far from being a cloistered spot where he can contemplate his model or his apple in peace. It is besieged by voices, all disturbing, some for one reason, some for another. First there is the voice which cries: "I cannot protect you; I cannot pay you. I am so tortured and distracted that I can no longer enjoy your works of art." Then there is the voice which asks for help. "Come down from your ivory tower, leave your studio," it cries, "and use your gifts as doctor, as teacher, not as artist." Again there is the voice which warns the artist that unless he can show good cause why art benefits the state he will be made to help it actively—by making aeroplanes, by firing guns. And finally there is the voice which many artists in other countries have already heard and had to obey—the voice which proclaims that the artist is the servant of the politician. "You shall only practise your art", it says, "at our bidding. Paint us pictures, carve us statues that glorify our gospels. Celebrate fascism; celebrate communism. Preach what we bid you preach. On no other terms shall you exist."

With all these voices crying and conflicting in his ears, how can the artist still remain at peace in his studio, contemplating his model or his apple in the cold light that comes through the studio window? He is forced to take part in politics; he must form himself into societies like the Artists' International Association. Two causes of supreme importance to him are in peril. The first is his own survival; the other is the survival of his art.

Royalty

To begin with a quotation, since it may throw light upon a very complex emotion: the accused came to town because, he said, "I wanted to see the Dukes and Kings."

The accused also said: "The inner man tells me that I am a Duke." Appearances were against him, and, as he had brought a pistol with him, his further actions took him to the Law Courts. But save that he went a step further than most of us, his state of mind was much the same as ours. We too want to see the Dukes and Kings. There is no denying it, for the picture papers show us what we want to see, and the picture papers are full of Dukes and Kings. Even at times which it is sufficient to call "like these" there are the little girls feeding the sea lions; there is the elderly lady accepting a bouquet; there is the young man with a ribbon across his breast. And we look at them, almost every day we look at them, because we too want to see the Dukes and Kings.

It is not a simple wish. It is very very old, to begin with, and old emotions like old families have intermarried and have many connections. Love of Royalty, or to give it its crude name, snobbery, is related to love of pageantry, which has some connection with love of beauty—a respectable connection; and again with the imagination—which is still more respectable for it creates poems and novels. Certainly an old body in black with a pair of horn spectacles on her nose required a good deal of gilding by the imagination before she became the British Empire personified. Scott undoubtedly had to use the same imagination upon George the Fourth's tumbler to make it worth stealing that he had to use upon the Waverley Novels to make them worth reading. We must call up battles and banners and many ghosts and glories before we see whatever it is that we do see in the picture of a child feeding a bear with a bun. But perhaps the most profound satisfaction that Royalty

Written in 1939

183

provides is that it gives us a Paradise to inhabit, and one much more domestic than that provided by the Church of England. Pile carpets are more palpable than fields of asphodel, and the music of the Scots Greys more audible than the hymns angels play upon their harps. Moreover, real people live in Buckingham Palace, but always smiling, perfectly dressed, immune, we like to imagine, if not from death and sorrow, still from the humdrum and the pettifogging. Even though our inner man does not tell us that we are Dukes, it is a consolation to know that such beings exist. If they live, then we too live in them, vicariously. Probably most people, as they hold out a penny to the bus conductor on a rainy night, have caught themselves pretending that a beautiful lady is stooping to kiss the royal hand, and the omnibus is lit up.

The last few years, however, have done some damage to this great Victorian dream. For as we know, the Dukes and Kings refused to play their part in the game any longer. Two at least declared that they had hearts like ours; one heart loved a Smith, the other a Simpson. The danger of this admission was at once felt to be very great. A leading statesman foraged in the College of Heralds and discovered that the lady was descended, perhaps on the mother's side, perhaps from a Knight, who had perhaps fought at the Battle of Hastings. But the public was not to be bamboozled. We said, we cannot dream our dreams about people with hearts like ours. Such names as Smith and Simpson rouse us to reality. And the emotion was finely discriminated by a Court lady, who said that though she could curtsey to Queen Elizabeth, the pink of grace and charm, there was a difference—precisely what, she omitted to say—between the curtsey she dropped an Earl's daughter and the curtsey she gave Queen Mary the Royal. As for bending to a name which is to be read in large letters over a well-known shop in Piccadilly, her knees, she said, positively and, as it appeared, quite independently of their owner, refused to comply.

Enough has been said to show that the matter is complex. Further, blue blood by itself is not enough. For though there are extreme Royalists who can sustain themselves upon the shades of the Stuarts—do they not still come with their white roses to the Martyr's grave?—the cruder mass of us requires that Royalty shall have its crown and sceptre. In France for example there are princes of the Houses of Bourbon and Orleans whose blood is perhaps bluer than that of our own House of Windsor. But nobody cares to see them feeding pandas. No photographs of them appear in the French picture papers. Snobbery, it seems, can get no nourishment from the stout man in a frock coat, who is the present King of France, because he has lost his palace and his crown. It is like feeding upon a painted rose. Off it flits, this queer human sensibility, in search of other food. Food it must have since it is alive and has been nourished, one way or another, ever since Hengist or Horsa, many centuries ago, made some old tin vessel serve for a crown. In France, as every traveller knows, it has found a substitute. It feeds not upon Royalty but upon religion; not indeed upon those ardours and ecstasies which are the kernel, but upon the husks and pageantry. It feeds upon processions and images; upon wayside shrines; on the holy man in cloth of gold blessing the fishing-boat; on children in white muslin; on the penny candles and the incense. The Roman Catholic religion provides with this pageantry a substitute for Royalty. It gives the poorest old crone, who has nothing but a bunch of roses to stick in a pot, something to dream about, and, what is equally important, something to do.

The English religion, however, whether because of the climate or because of the creed, has nothing of the kind to offer. It is a black and white indoor affair which makes no appeal to our senses and asks no help from our hands. If therefore Royalty fails to gratify our need of Royalty, the Protestant religion is not going to come to our help. The desire will have to find some other outlet. And the picture papers, in which we see the reflection of so many desires, are already hinting at a possible substitute. At present it is a hint only, and a very humble hint—nothing more than a caterpillar. It is true that it was a rare caterpillar; a gentleman in Kensington had found it in his back garden. And so it had its photograph in the news, and appeared almost life-size upon the very same page as the picture of the Princess who was feeding the panda. There they were, side by side. But what is important is that the eye, passing from the Princess to the caterpillar, registered a thrill which, though different from the Royalty thrill, was like enough to serve much the same purpose. The desire of the moth for the star was gratified by the caterpillar. How wonderful are caterpillars—so we may translate that thrill—symmetrical in shape and brilliantly barred; the Privet Hawk wears, not one garter ribbon across its breast, but three or four. How little—the thrill continued—we know of the lives of caterpillars, living mysteriously on the heights of elm trees; urged by instincts that are not ours; immune from worry; and capable, as we are not, of putting off this gross body and winging their way . . . in short, the caterpillar suggested that if a mere caterpillar found in Kensington can cause this thrill (here curtailed) and if this thrill is much the same as that which Royalty used to provide when Royalty was barred and beautiful and immune from human weakness, then perhaps Science will do instead. There is in being, if at present only in germ, some curiosity about this unknown world that might be fed. This unknown world is after all more beautiful than Buckingham Palace, and its inhabitants will never, in all probability, come down from the tree-top to mate with the Smiths and the Simpsons. If the picture papers then would come to our help, we might dream a new dream, acquire a new snobbery; we might see the coral insect at work; the panda alone in his forest; the wild yet controlled dance of the atoms which makes, it is said, the true being of the kitchen table; and spend our curiosity upon them. The camera has an immense power in its eye, if it would only turn that eye in rather a different direction. It might wean us by degrees from the Princess to the panda, and shunt us past religion to pay homage to Science, as some think a more venerable royal house than the House of Windsor. Above all it could check the most insidious and dangerous of current snobberies, which is making the workers into Kings; has invested the slum, the mine, and the factory with the old glamour of the palace, so that, as modern fiction shows, we are beginning to escape, by picturing the lives of the poor and day-dreaming about them, from the drudgery, about which there is no sort of glamour, of being ourselves.

Royalty

MANY important autobiographies have appeared this autumn, but none stranger or in certain respects more interesting than *The Story of My Life*, by Marie, Queen of Roumania. The reasons seem to be that she is royal; that she can write; that no royal person has ever been able to write before; and that the consequences may well be extremely serious.

Royalty to begin with, merely as an experiment in the breeding of human nature, is of great psychological interest. For centuries a certain family has been segregated; bred with a care only lavished upon race-horses; splendidly housed, clothed, and fed; abnormally stimulated in some ways, suppressed in others; worshipped, stared at, and kept shut up, as lions and tigers are kept, in a beautiful brightly lit room behind bars. The psychological effect upon them must be profound; and the effect upon us is as remarkable. Sane men and women as we are, we cannot rid ourselves of the superstition that there is something miraculous about these people shut up in their cage. Common sense may deny it; but take common sense for a walk through the streets of London on the Duke of Kent's wedding-day. Not only will he find himself in a minority, but as the gold coach passes and the bride bows, his hand will rise to his head; off will come his hat, or on the contrary it will be rammed firmly on his head. In either case he will recognise the divinity of royalty.

Now one of these royal animals, Queen Marie of Roumania, has done what had never been done before; she has opened the door of the cage and sauntered out into the street. Queen Marie can write; in a second, therefore, the bars are down. Instead of the expected suavities and sweetnesses we come upon sharp little words; Uncle Bertie laughs, "his laugh was a sort of crackle"; Kitty Renwick kept the medicine chest; "the castor oil pills looked like transparent white grapes with the oil moving about

Written in 1939

187

inside"; there were "little squares of burnt skin" on the pudding at Windsor; Queen Victoria's teeth were "small like those of a mouse"; she had a way of shrugging her shoulders when she laughed; when they rode on the sands at evening "the shadows become so long that it is as though our horses were walking on stilts"; there was a marvellous stone in the museum, like a large piece of shortbread, that "swayed slightly up and down when held at one end". This little girl, in short, smelt, touched, and saw as other children do; but she had an unusual power of following her feeling until she had coined the word for it. That is to say, she can write.

If we want an example of the difference between writing and non-writing we have only to compare a page of Queen Marie with a page of Queen Victoria. The old Queen was, of course, an author. She was forced by the exigencies of her profession to fill an immense number of pages, and some of these have been printed and bound between covers. But between the old Queen and the English language lay an abyss which no depth of passion and no strength of character could cross. Her works make very painful reading on that account. She has to express herself in words; but words will not come to her call. When she feels strongly and tries to say so, it is like hearing an old savage beating with a wooden spoon on a drum. " . . . this last refusal of Servia . . . almost *forces us* to SEE *that* there is *no* false play." Rhythm is broken; the few poverty-stricken words are bruised and battered; now hooked together with hyphens, now desperately distended with italics and capital letters—it is all no good. In the same way her descriptions of celebrated people slip through the fingers like water. "I waited a moment in the Drawing-room to speak to Irving and Ellen Terry. He is very gentleman-like, and she, very pleasing and handsome." This primitive little machine is all that she has with which to register some of the most extraordinary experiences that ever fell to a woman's lot. But probably she owed much of her prestige to her inability to express herself. The majority of her subjects, knowing her through her writing, came to feel that only a woman immune from the usual frailties and passions of human nature could write as Queen Victoria wrote. It added to her royalty.

But now by some freak of fate, which Queen Victoria would have been the first to deplore, her granddaughter, the eldest child of the late Duke and Duchess of Edinburgh, has been born with a pen in her hand. Words do her bidding. Her own account of it is illuminating: "Even as a child", she says, "I possessed a vivid imagination and I liked telling stories to my sisters. . . . Then one of my children said to me: 'Mama, you ought to write all this down, it is a pity to allow so many beautiful pictures to fade away'. . . . I knew nothing whatever about writing, about style or composition, or about the 'rules of the game', but I did know how to conjure up beauty, also at times, emotion. I also had a vast store of words." It is true; she knows nothing about "the rules of the game"; words descend and bury whole cities under them; sights that should have been seen once and for all are distracted and dissipated; she ruins her effects and muffs her chances; but still because she feels abundantly, because she rides after her emotion fearlessly and takes her fences without caring for falls, she conjures up beauty and conveys emotion. Nor is it merely that by a happy fluke she is able to hit off a moment's impression, a vivid detail; she has the rarer power of sweeping these figures along in a torrent of language; lives grow and change beneath our eyes; scenes form themselves; details arrange themselves; all the actors come alive. Her most remarkable achievement in this way is her portrait of "Aunty"—that Queen Elizabeth of Roumania who called herself Carmen Sylva. As it happened, Queen Victoria also tried her hand at a portrait of this lady. "The dear charming Queen", she writes, "came to luncheon. . . . She spoke with resignation and courage of her many trials and difficulties. . . . I gave her a Celtic brooch and Balmoral shawl, also some books. . . . The Queen read to us one of her plays, an ancient Greek story, very tragic. She read it to us most wonderfully and beautifully, and had quite an inspired look as she did so. . . . Many could, of course, not understand, as she read it in German, but all were interested."

In Queen Marie's hands this "dear charming Queen" develops out of all recognition. She becomes a complex contradictory human being, wearing floating veils and a motoring cap, at once "splendid and absurd". We see her posing in bed under a top light; dramatising herself melodramatically; luxuriating in the flattery of sycophants; declaiming poetry through a megaphone to ships at sea; waving a napkin to grazing cows whom she mistakes for loyal subjects—deluded and fantastic, but at the same time generous and sincere. So the picture shapes itself, until all the different elements are shown in action. Two scenes stand out with genuine vitality— one where the romantic impulsive old lady seeks to enchant an ancient flame—the late Duke of Edinburgh—by dragging him to a hill-top where hidden minstrels spring out from behind rocks and bawl native melodies into his disgusted ears; the other where Queen Elizabeth of Roumania and Queen Emma of Holland sit at their needlework while the Italian secretary reads aloud. He chose Maeterlinck, and as he declaimed the famous passage where the queen bee soars higher and higher in her nuptial ecstasy till at last the male insect, ravaged by passion, drops dismembered to the ground, Carmen Sylva raised her beautiful white hands in rapture. But Queen Emma gave one look at the reader and went on hemming her duster.

Vivid as it all is, nobody is going to claim that Queen Marie ranks with Saint Simon or with Proust. Yet it would be equally absurd to deny that by virtue of her pen she has won her freedom. She is no longer a royal queen in a cage. She ranges the world, free like any other human being to laugh, to scold, to say what she likes, to be what she is. And if she has escaped, so too, thanks to her, have we. Royalty is no longer quite royal. Uncle Bertie, Onkel, Aunty, Nando, and the rest, are not mere effigies bowing and smiling, opening bazaars, expressing exalted sentiments, and remembering faces always with the same sweet smile. They are violent and eccentiric; charming and ill-tempered; some have bloodshot eyes; others handle flowers with a peculiar tenderness. In short, they are very like ourselves. They live as we do. And the effect is surprising. A month or two ago, the late Duke of Edinburgh was as dead as the dodo. Now, thanks to his daughter, we know that he liked beer; that he liked to sip it while he read his paper; that he hated music; that he loathed Roumanian melodies; and that he sat on a rock in a rage.

But what will be the consequences if this familiarity between them and us increases? Can we go on bowing and curtseying to people who are just like ourselves? Are we not already a little ashamed of the pushing and the staring now that we know from these two stout volumes that one at least of the animals can talk? We begin to wish that the Zoo should be abolished; that the royal animals should be given the run of some wider pasturage—a royal Whipsnade. And another question suggests itself. When a gift for writing lodges in a family, it often persists and improves; and if Queen Marie's descendants improve upon her gift as much as she has improved upon Queen Victoria's is it not quite possible that a real poet will be King of England in a hundred years time? And suppose that among the autumn books of 2034 is *Prometheus Unbound*, by George the Sixth, or *Wuthering Heights*, by Elizabeth the Second, what will be the effect upon their loyal subjects? Will the British Empire survive? Will Buckingham Palace look as solid then as it does now? Words are dangerous things, let us remember. A republic might be brought into being by a poem.